The Mansion Gardens

ISBN 1-905168-11-X
First Edition

Published by Paula Brown Publishing 2006

Copyright © Alan Morrison 2006
Copyright © Paula Brown 2006

Alan Morrison has asserted his legal right under the Copyright, Designs and Patents Act 1988 to be identified as the writer of this work. The copyright for the cover design illustration remains with Alan Morrison and the design with Yann Pitchal

This book is sold subject to the condition that it shall not be lent, resold, hired out or otherwise circulated without the publisher's written consent in any other form of binding or cover other than that in which it is published and without a similar condition being imposed on the subsequent purchaser.

First published in the UK by
Paula Brown Publishing
www.paulabrownpublishing.com
www.thepeoplespoet.com

A CIP catalogue record for this book is available from the British Library.

Printed and bound in Great Britain by
The Basingstoke Press

The Mansion Gardens

Alan Morrison

Forgive-Me-Not

Let go. Forgive. Forget the bitterness
That buttresses when love is dead:
Most of what's said isn't meant;
Most of what's meant isn't said.

*This collection is dedicated to my parents Andrew and Helen,
and Lucía, mi flor silvestre.*

'But I don't allow it's luck and all a toss;
There's no such thing as being starred and crossed;
It's just the power of some to be a boss,
And the bally power of others to be bossed...'

John Davidson,
'Thirty Bob A Week'

Contents

Front poem: Forgive-Me-Not

Foreword 9

Poems 1991 – 2006 13

Keir Hardie Street 150

Index 169

Acknowledgements 171

Final poem: Giving Light

Foreword

Alan Morrison is an extraordinary poet born for 1974. Reading him, you might think the poetry was written by someone active in 1974, though the language and poetics have clearly been rinsed in the decades that succeeded this. And the poetry is far finer than the average kind of polemical writing that Morrison has wedded his own gifts to. As a poet he is rooted in acute historicisms as well as a throbbing sense of what it is like writing as a convinced and historically aware Socialist in the early 21st century – indeed, exactly 100 years on from when one of his heroes, Robert Tressell started writing his great working-class novel, *The Ragged Trousered Philanthropists*.

Poverty, family, Socialism, Catholicism often crop up (literally) in Morrison's work like stones in a garden of verses. This is unfashionable. There's a burdened obsessiveness with these themes in Morrison's writing, the kind that generates most real poetry. Themes like these currently marginalise anyone writing within them. Morrison is inordinate and alone as Tim Allen once said of Andrew Duncan in a similar context. He's also extremely bloody-minded and cannot rid himself of his themes. Nor does he attempt to diversify into sexier workshop-aided delicacies. He is perennially one might put it workshop-shy and would only tell you to hark back to the iniquities when English was hammered out through the workshop of the world.

His poetry though inhabits its own linguistic parabulia of obsession, crisis and occasionally Hardy-esque resolution. Morrison tends to the confessional long poem, not something that socialists are encouraged to indulge in. Indeed, Morrison's own obsessions cut across the very socialisms they promulgate. There is in a strict sense an indulgence in non-indulgence which operates as a compulsive reordering of the emotions generated, rather than putting on a face of purposeful optimism but the degree to which Morrison examines and excoriates the conditions of his own and his family's life, as well as other fantasias involving sympathetic alter-egos and sub-heroes, is quite unflinching. It takes in fact an extraordinary degree of courage to write such confessional poetry striated with such a Socialist edge. The themes itch against each other, one confessional, the other tight-lipped and thrusting such confessions away to quickly resolve personal difficulties without recourse to quite so many words. This tension makes Morrison's poetry quite unique and explains why the courage, often visibly painful, is not foolhardiness.

Morrison's poetic strategies take their bearings from several distinct sources, perhaps more than any other poet, John Davidson's influence (particularly in 'Thirty Bob a Week' and also in the later Testaments) have clearly enthused Morrison's exactingly dour yet exhilarating details as well as occasionally his rhythmic inflections. Other poets like the more polemically-edged Romantics and above all Harold Monro, have sharpened the melancholia in his palette. Monro's sense of transience and halfway houses of recovery and damnation have bitten into Morrison's elegiac language like nothing else. If Monro as Eliot said of him 'has done what no other poet has done at all', then Morrison has done with Monro what no other poet has done or would dare to do with him. The curl and slap of Morrison's own particularity, his twitch disturbing Monro's onerously 'Silent Pool', is hauntingly memorable.

Monro lived as Eliot generously acknowledged on the cusp of Modernism; also, as Pound wrote to him in a letter, Monro was too generous to his fellow Georgians, promoting far too much 'second-rate lopp'. Certain of his poems don't escape a mild Georgian basileus rather as if he had left 'Milk for the Cat' out for a little too long. Morrison's Georgian tendencies are however not so personally sentimentalised as having Edward Carpenter (the famous Socialist poet) calling round on Monro in his sandals. Morrison shares nothing of the strangeness of certain of Monro's states, for instance, the wise desolation of 'Bitter Sanctuary' (but for stylistic influence see 'Infatuation: The First'). This, hewn out of earlier Georgian expansions, is the kind of poem which begins to emerge, roughcast, out of some of Morrison's desolate elegies ('The Cottage', 'The House of Sadness Past' and the epic 'Clocking-in for the Witching Hour' etc.). This attunement is where Morrison and Monro show their most natural affinity: isolation. It is not that self-excoriating isolation and hallucinated uniqueness of sensibility that produced, for instance, 'Overheard on a Saltmarsh' – that has a wildness and amused self-pitying tang that would be impossible to emulate, and even if it were, not desirable, except to the inveterately gothic. Morrison's unique voice is attuned more to the special melancholia that fuels the best of Monro; not the explorations of the latter's own haunted sexuality and alcoholism. Lucky for Morrison.

Morrison's poetry is not only like no other, it could never be so even if it tried. This is a test of true poetry. His language is by turns concise and honed in the lyrics and contoured with a curious lope of its own in the longer works.

Comparisons have been made to John Clare's nakedness of spirit. There's an affinity like slantwise rain to Alun Lewis, which is all in the tone and tangency of the writing and metre. There are of course signposts in a poet's development and the genuine awkwardness of somebody finding their own and not an easy contemporary way. Morrison's impulse is to build up, say like Montale (in Italian) not again like Ungaretti – the contrast is instructive. His partner is Spanish, and Spanish poets, too, though not the obvious models, have inflected his output. Most of all, though, try the imagined retro-Edwardian fantasies in a later city of dreadful nights ('Keir Hardie Street'). It shows the way he might develop. And Morrison is still developing quite rapidly; has not learnt except startlingly in a few poems and lines that luminosity won after an enormous poetic tension has been resolved, merely to reinvest itself in its own obsessions. But he's getting there; and a full volume is certainly due, if not exactly overdue, since he's still in his early thirties. And this decade remains rather a good one for the extermination of premature talents. His own gifts however are likely to endure.

Simon Jenner
February 2006

The conflict between the poet and the performer is something Alan is confronting in all his work. His working through producing one pamphlet after another is a powerful and deceptively simple way of confronting the truth that is his own and nobody else's. We have areas of interest in common; we both love the work of Stevie Smith, a Poet and Performer who only really entered the public arena in the Sixties through her association with the likes of Adrian Mitchell et al.; we both suffer from OCD (obsessive-compulsive disorder); and above all we are both indefatigable seekers after the truth that is uniquely ours. I believe, with more and more successful performances of his play for voices, *Picaresque* (see the favourable notice in the *Guardian Review* of Saturday December 17, 2005), Alan will write more and more for the stage. I shall be very surprised if this play isn't broadcast on Radio 4 in the near future.

He is a lot tougher and tenderer in all his work confronting what many poets would run a million miles from confronting. OCD is a particularly vexatious way of being made to go through life and Alan daily faces incredible challenges by producing works at the same time as editing other peoples' and the Survivors' Poetry magazine, *Poetry Express*. Through all his work Alan is an indefatigable seeker – both with a Blakean and Stevie Smith-type vision; it's the conflict between how he would like his life to be and how it really is that produces the great diversification of his work. Indeed, some of Alan's epigrams have a Blakean feeling pulsating right the way through them. Every word counts. The poems, in their quirkiness, also remind me of Stevie.

Productivity in published poets and writers is often most unfairly sneered at – there is a great deal to be said in producing work in the way Alan does. It is the trial and error way and will help him to reach audiences he deserves through his great gifts as a poet and performer. He may not resolve that conflict – it is in fact his greatest ally.

    John Horder
    January 2006

Alan Morrison has a 'voice' ("All that poets can have", as Auden said) and one entirely his own; electric. Seeing the 'specialness' inherent in ordinary phenomena is the essence of the poet's art and the unfolding of his personal 'take' is the principal delight of reading good work. Morrison does not flinch about 'coming out' as a sufferer from obsessive compulsive disorder: for this too he deserves the high praise his poetry demands. His work is an interesting mixture of innocence and experience.

Stanza 4 of 'Last of the Spray Carnations' is worthy of Pound. 'Tears of mustard sun'– I wish I'd written that! The shorter poems too are excellent – wise, witty and full of feeling. 'The Cottage' is marvellous. At 63 when I read his work I feel there's hope for poetry still.

Morrison is a hope for English poetry where hope is in short supply.

    Barry Tebb
    2005

The Water Shallows

As I was paddling in the water shallows,
the ripples turned to waves,
the paddling to a wade.

While I tried to shallow my tumbling mind,
the thoughts that swam in the water shallows
were chased as fish by the shadows of sparrows

Nostalgia

Even in those golden days
Life always left us wanting more –
Why we loathe ourselves today
Is why we loved ourselves before.

The House on the Rise of Reversion

Regarding the house on the rise,
Shabby, ramshackle, severe,
Of crabby stone and rustic gate,
Subjective views judge here.

Eyes entirely detached survey
A shambling garden with scorn –
Instead of empathising they
Petition us to cut the lawn.

Greeted by a worn, cracked face
A visitor digs up a dearth
Of signatures – Dad's trampled eyes
Displace the criticising earth.

Threats delivered, the visitor leaves.
An anxious face of thwarted youth
Twitches through reclusive curtains,
Haunting a window's hidden truth.

Inside: a tea-dripped radiator;
Kipling's If on a blanched wall fades
In a crack of sunlight through a broken pane:
Hide for spying listing spades.

Outside: a shoddy wire enclosure
Mangy guards limply patrol,
Possessive of a callous house –
Snouts in empty tins, they troll.

Forsythia's golden petals glow
Defiant, alone; the colour; the hope;
The island of life in a rough sea of weeds
Willing the rubble-bed garden to cope.

The Mansion Gardens

Shall we stroll those mansion gardens,
baize on baize of velvet grass
so well-kept and un-walked-upon?
Come on, love, we've cut the coupons,
let's see those shouting flowers
round grounds of ivy towers.

Shall we walk those mansion cloisters
verged with portraits? There's the Lords
and Ladies, and their ancestors
hanging, framed and ashen-faced.

But why are they ashen-faced dear,
when they lived respectfully here?

Shall we stroll those dust-still rooms –
well, just alongside, take a little
look at them, just peep inside?
They're cordoned-off with red rope...

just like our lives...

oh, we'll cope.

Shall we pace those mansion chambers
ringed by pasty-plaited rope...

easily unhooked and disobeyed...

No – that would be to abandon
our law-abiding principles...

what's wrong is always irresistible...

Shall we recall those mansion gardens,

baize on baize of velvet grass
so well-kept and un-walked-upon?

I'm not envious: simply a dreamer:
those lawns seemed so much greener...

Make Way

Make Way! their banners gallop
In the choppy Cornish wind;
'He Lives! He Lives!' crashes on cramped
Coverack, Lilliput-twinned.

On the craggy harbour-side
They rejoice their Saviour's Risen!
And yet He's still invisible,
While their clammed evangelism

Is vivid and immovable
As Coverack shacks' limpet-cling
To granite rocks; or barnacles
On the moored hull of *Tamarind*.

Rustling tambourines displace
The shingle's cymbal hissing –
No footprints to be made out on
The sand because the tide is in.

In Chapel they all clap their hands,
Sing with palms splayed up in prayer
Spun by a cardigan-man on guitar
Strumming in a thumping chair.

In among the rocking pews
The Not-Yet-Born-Again's found out;
Someone nudges me: 'Come on,
Clap!' – the spell to cast off doubt?

Into the street they pour their peal
Pounding on my doubting brow –
Bashing tambourines they dash
My faith like fish-brains on a bow.

The Corn Thresher

1
I gather the corn-strands from the field,
bind them together to force them to yield.
My act is assertion of mastery
over my nature – whatever that be.

2
A Confucian in my down-cast stare,
all green without spoil seems barren and bare
to my tampering eyes and grappling hands
that wrestle with Nature till She understands.

3
Onto my threshing-floor I step
binding tighter my thoughts like old men, regrets –
or confessing Catholics the sums of sins
their intermediary's stale ear wins.

4
Then I wield my flail for the threshing
like the Father incense for blessing
the echoing house of his God on high,
to fumigate and purify.

5
When the job's almost done I grip
the bound corn tight in my fingertips
and perform the threshing manually –
with my chore I achieve true harmony.

6
My eyes, full of purpose as bales of hay,
roll about with an impulse like clouds during day,
as the grains of corn sheaves spill out free
like beads from a broken rosary.

7
I am a thresher of the corn
working the field in the chilly dawn,
I bind my thoughts tight in Belief
and thrash out all the grains of grief.

8
With every thresh of the flail I delve
into the Truth gripped in the helve;
my binding my thoughts is my will to believe
I shall resurrect like corn from its sheave.

Dole and Genealogy

1
The fireplace littered with Carlsberg cans
he sits, disconsolate.
Concentration fills his hands:
his hobby gropes to compensate
for his neglected state.

From chair to chair he'll stumble
mapping out ancestral pasts;
in fogs of nostalgia he'll fumble
through fictitious fasts.
Traces the line the light casts.

Dimming light. Dull evening glow
displays his only pride:
ancestors' names, row on row,
dead before his time although
he feels they're tutting by his side

judging him. Tries to appease
their disappointment in him
by tracing ad infinitum
far into his fantasies,
fizzing cans, full ashtrays.

2
I find him foraging for childhood,
sleep-lost in stolen pasts
where memory graves are his mind-food
for hope; stale bread that lasts
till shattered like plaster-casts.

What use is love? Over us looms
a quiet Catholic God, aloof
from our penniless misfortunes,
old invisible heirlooms

flogged long ago to keep this roof
of poverty's brooding proof.

Can I convince my maltreated father
God is on our side
when our cramped prayers have scrimped an after
of comfortless dark?   Time and tide
long passed on the other side.

In creeps a torrid afternoon
of brief self-pitying;
more motherless sobs fill the room,
nothing can lift the casting of gloom
over the sound of a grown man crying.

3
I pity the prowess with which he heaps
more shame upon himself
as he lumbers his dad's damp-blotched books
onto the listing shelf –
sad tributes to a faded wealth.

More than any other member
of his leafless family tree
he personifies the motto
Forgetful Of One's Own Interests
warped through verdigris.

'I've done my duty, I'd done my best'
he mutters to a mirror
repeating this and all the rest
that still he is no winner
but definitely a sinner –
always self-accuser, never self-forgiver.

4
He slips to sleep and dreams of more
sleep; cuts adrift from the shore

of consciousness.   The more he copes
the more he reeks of cigarette smoke
that fogs the fact his nerves are broke –

and what chance did his nerves have
when at the age of three his skin
was blistered to the third degree?
Sixty years on his hands aren't ready
to keep their cigarette fingers steady.

I see his eyes are blurring again
back to blood-shot bleariness,
tired whites slowly yellowing –
I see him trace the family name
back to the safety of the past –
but how long can nostalgia last?

...long as lamplight puddles pages
of photocopied parish records
he trains his straining sights towards –
as the light begins to fail
his mind will slowly gather sail
and trace the print like mental Braille.

In the dark, he'll bite his nails.

A Summer Night's Travels

i. on embarking

in a stale airless bedroom
she lay white as sand
on rock-pools of crumpled bed-clothes

through tousling cigarette smoke
I sailed to her side,
smoked with her a while,
stroked her bare leg noticing
the structure of her smile

she found my smooth hand pleasing,
I, her pleasing stare,
for once I felt unembarrassed
travelling down there;

in love with innocence of touch:
(instinct's simplicity sent ashore
with straying hands):

infatuated with the tangible side of desire:

fingertips interpreting
goose-pimple braille indenting
shining moisturised skin...

ii. the calm

I snuggled closer to her
under blankets, fathoming
for sexless moments, satisfied
with just mattering...

iii. the storm

clambered to her mouth,
prised her lips, sampling
salt taste, warm pepper breath

her tongue was swelling like a whelk
inside its shell

I burrowed down to berth
in clammy shallows

she rose to sink her coral teeth
in my crow's neck,   sank back
into the bruise of night

I keeled onto my side –
she reared up like a wave
dashed herself on deck...

iv. the wreck

undercurrents stir the wreck
of twisted bed-sheets,
tissues tentacle like seaweed flames...

memories limpet the mind
in tides of minutes,
fill the sooty hold with split
licks of spitting fire...

infatuated with the tangible side of desire...

The China Kingfisher

Dubbed useless for most of his days,
He saw himself in a similar light.
Counted hours in the window's haze;
Inert; a bird without flight.

Time tapered by, lost to a chair,
The nest from which he's seldom stirred;
From a window-ledge he flies the air
In an ornament shaped as a bird.

Imagines the wings that spirit away
Wishes set free from the mind of the wisher;
Pictures a lake on a still summer's day,
And flitting about it, a China Kingfisher.

Few Never Envy

All I have: this shabby room
furnished grandma-style:
carpet muddy umber,
thin beige curtains pile
like luminous mosquito nets
over the draughty window-pane.
A lacquered table's centre-piece
where I eat cold meals, scrimp an aim

inkling in a typewriter.
Plastic clatter of tone-deaf keys
scores each curtained, fiction-night:
a blind mind tinkling ivories.
Breaks spent on a spineless bed;
fingers brush the woodchip Braille,
step across the blue-tack path,
trip to creak of banister-rail.

I stare up at a blanched Van Gogh
by the toothpaste-spattered sink;
the ticking of the crippled clock
decides it isn't time to think;
I rise to wash: chalky water
chokes out to the rusty squeak
of the stiffer tap; over my shoulder
a back-to-front Thirty Bob A Week

reflects in the mirror that traps me.
Smoking soothes as doubts unroll.
My only other luxuries: tea
and sleeping pills when I get my dole
of hardship maintenance that feeds
my lapsed Protestant shame
(though I was born a Catholic
I'm English all the same).

Few never envy others' lives
with their ambitions in arrears;
only thoughts that telescope
help one cope – focused years
blur the edges of fogged progress.
Lungs fangled for spearmint fags
purse their pockets. Abstracts heap
like half-p's in the money bags.

Destiny

She's push-chaired in on every shift
by a mother who sighs with coffee sips
cauterizing suicide no doubt
or some other similar way out:
a bit more brown, another score
might push things on a little more.

Destiny sits there taking it in
with rag-doll's eyes, still, unblinking;
eyes no child should see with; no shine;
a grubby-faced Little Mother Time,
her mother's troubles sitting
on her marble brow's dark knitting.

I search for some sign in her eyes
of something like infant surprise
but the sharps of her mind are cluttered up
with images of her mother jacking up
in nightly attempts to numb the pain
coursing through syringe-thin vein.

Does Destiny deserve her name?

A Day at the Council Estates

We took part in a car-boot sale
to flog some old toys for our lack of money;
forced by circumstance to compromise
our impoverished principles, capitalise
on this opportunity in the council estates,
we touted our out-dated merchandise.

But father, no salesman, bit his lip
as he witnessed the scruffy kids stare in awe
at chipped Britains' soldiers and Star Wars figures
their frustrated parents couldn't afford –
we wanted to give them away there and then,
but poverty pressed us to set up a pitch.

Stood gormless in labyrinths of open boots,
prised oysters on a shabby asphalt bed
of playground, I saw a grubby child tugging
his father's sleeve, eyes glued to our toys
like price tags. Something died in me then:
I couldn't believe in anything again.

Seemed to me truth was cheap and nasty
like the plastic toys we recycled for sale
and I felt crippled with sympathy
for a child who was wearing old jumble-sale clothes,
a urine-stained t-shirt and filthy corduroys,
who knows all he sees, and sees all he knows.

My Life in the Shade

Since I was sunburnt as a boy I learnt to love the shade,
Spared me from the heat where the other children played –
But I was tugged out in the sun and punished by its light
Turning from a shadow to someone in my own right,
Found that I'd preferred it when I'd felt invisible.
Sometimes I wonder whether I was ever here at all.

I've always loved so easily and pitied anyone
Who showed signs of remorse for the wrongs that they had done.
I've struggled and I've buckled under every thought I've had
As if the mere imagining of bad events was bad;
Pursued by Furies of my own phantasmagorical school.
Sometimes I wonder whether I was ever here at all.

The more I've lived I've lost myself and drifted far away
From the busy worlds of others and the places where they play.
As if I died some time ago and turned into a ghost
Haunting all the places that I used to love the most,
I've lingered like a shadow where my own shadow should fall.
Sometimes I wonder whether I was ever here at all.

I came to fear feelings of love for how they made me see
The image of myself through the eyes of those who loved me.
Until I was obsessed with being gone in all but mind
Sharing in the mourning with my loved ones left behind.
But I'm still here; still in the shade; trembling in its thrall.
Sometimes I wonder whether I was ever here at all.

Tales from the Empty Larder

I can't stand scant catechisms
of tremors in an empty stomach;
the stench of hunger-scented breath
where a full belly's the only tonic;
the famished itch in-between the teeth
where only food can feed relief.

The stain won't shift: mean-spirited strife
spoilt my appetite for living well;
splintered my spittle with bitterness;
chipped my shoulder with its scrimping chisel -
I taste it still in weak stewed blends;
in sickly stings of singed dog-ends.

I suppose the harsh lessons I scribed
inspired in me a need to dream,
to believe in insubstantial truths,
for you need a God when you can't keep clean
and hope, when your faith overspills,
socialism will cure most ills.

But it's often the morbid human way
to come to love what you should despise
just as, in depression, sadness comforts
with blessings of tears in tea-strained eyes;
so I feel perverse nostalgia
for those hours of hunger-fed neuralgia.

I've said to my brother, it's strange to think
amid the dirt we found ideals,
a sense of justice in second-hand clothes
and transubstantiated packet meals –
the dark of a larder's empty shelves:
where we first found ourselves.

The Cottage

For all the breath-smoked winter nights
we shared some misty summers
drifting off to light tunes' fall
like balsam on the garden
from my brother's bedroom window
jarred with grandma's *Iliad;*
sunbathed with mongrels at our feet;
plucked blushed apples from the tree beside
the cement-filled well, where we planted
hope for rescue from this rustic lull
false as our restless wishes were,
still yet to be weeded.

Father's face hair-line cracked
as the crumbly stone of the cottage walls;
mother's nerves fragile as
the shaky glass of the greenhouse grave –
I'm sure she's shrunken in this shade
all these faded years;
given the choice she wouldn't leave
this place for ties still tested like
the trembling washing-line.

This is where we dug-up doubt
fossilized in the outhouse stone
like stories of our mythical home;
where we first came to believe
in not believing, with the countryside,
that simply is. How could we leave.

Old-Fashioned Sun

Eleven years old, I tried to reclaim
the past, inspired by a cottage's gloom –
the countryside is always the same
no matter what year: I furnished my room
with my dad's dog-eared books caked in damp-stain
from *The Black Arrow* to *Allan Quatermain*.

On brumal mornings as a pale sun
lit thin curtains that filtered its rays,
I'd stick Holst's scratchy Jupiter on
summoning my father's schoolboy days –
Somerset, Nineteen Fifty-One,
in the ghostly warmth of an old-fashioned sun.

But there's a book-end to the shelf of time:
one can't stay absent from their age
in the fusty clutter of historic shrine –
so I parted the curtains, tripped the page
to the post-imperfect future time,
where pop lyrics strip the Kipling rhyme.

The Ring

No wizard there as our guide –
Poverty's spell casts all else to one side.
Father's face grey as Gandalf's gown.
He always told himself he'd let us down.

Love is its own darkness, slowly binding.

One day my mother had to pawn her ring,
But kept it secret till we'd finished eating;
Her finger as it was before their wedding.

A Hamper from Landrake

In the creel of a slate-skied Cornish winter
we caught a scraping sound outside;
a huge mass landing, heavy as the weight
my father prayed would be lifted from
his jobless shoulders scraped and bowed –

cold wind shot through the hallway, lo!
we beheld a hamper packed with tins
and vegetables – no Christians,
just a scribbled note blown on the lino
saying *from the Parish* – my father scowled,
now he was obliged to let them Save him.

Infatuation: The First

Infatuation? It didn't last
Beyond rosy, rough-and-tumble days,
Gooseberry sweet, no sour aftertaste.
Time didn't intimidate the infant; time was sky.
The love, the bond that tore our hearts
Strained too far, sighed out to die.

*Time's the face you love
but are tired of looking at.*

Bitterness of callow apples, raw,
Windfall-bitten, sour out the tongue
With immature spices to subtle in
Its un-acquired taste – sap squandered on
Those who sample before ripe; spat out;
Wiped clean by sleeves it bruises on.

*Time's a face you love
but tire of looking at.*

Time takes long to trickle on; to traipse.
Rich spit of first kisses infiltrates the rest.
He: *life's not long enough for love.*
She: *love purses lips for death;*
Familiarity and death: the same.
We tied knots in our stubborn bond; our breath.

*Time's a face you love
but are tired of looking at.*

Feelings home in unhealed sores;
In lichened ruins bonds re-build
On slippery foundations – love clings on;
No shutting off till we're told – mistakes,
Only palpable once trampled past,
Form the pattern of the human face.

*Time's the face you love
but tire of looking at.*

The False Confession

English Martyrs Primary School
Taught us hymns, Hail Marys, guilt;
On asphalt playgrounds, chalked pitches,
We played out innocence to the hilt.

One lunchtime, strayed to the other school
For spastic children, sat in class –
As I froze over a moment's thought
My friends face-aped them through the glass.

Walnut-faced Miss Wall called us
Into her plimsoll-smelling office;
Pitting us against each other
x2 chances to confess.

Five 'No's later, our only escape
From standing shame in assembly
Was for me to say Yes on their behalf
(A revelation to me).

Now I stood, the guilty of the three,
Accused of betrayal by the other two
By confessing to what I didn't do –
But who did I betray? Them or me?

The Rosary Beads

Dour Miss Wall casts dark on our
pale foreheads, fingers the rosary beads,
makes us chant a Hail Mary
for the rub of every wooden ball –
morning instruction in future obsession
at English Martyrs Primary School.

9 'o'clock cold polished floor
grounds our numbers' numb bums in
an overcast assembly hall;
Calvary clouds crowd the windows;
the dark jackdaws like a flock of crows.

Morning has broken…

pince-nez pinched, beak-nosed Miss Blades
perches like Professor Yaffle
at her wood bookend piano,
marches thimble fingers on
the thumping ivories…

He's got the whole world in his hands…

one hundred and something O-shaped mouths
chorus OHP-penned cant:

Do not be afraid…

The music dies; lift of spirits
sinks to sighs.

Miss Wall re-manifests, impresses
guilt, our holy catechism –
without speaking issues this instruction:
Question your desires.

My eyes restrain tears.
My thoughts leap back.
Each bead sticks in my throat,
imagining Hell's fires...

Candles and Anglicans

Father, the ethical, earthed C of E,
called us Roman Candles teasingly,
took his bread un-leavened;
spread butter on only one slice of his toast,
spared the other half austerely;
stuck Anglican rationality –

Mother, Obsessive-Confessive, prone
to genuflecting superstitions,
self-prescribed Lourdes' potions
for a phobia of pills –

but they shared one sparking trait:
waxen self-sacrificial wills.

A spark lit flames of Roman Candles;
two sons' indivisible aim
harmonised from sparring angles:
to make sense from a martyr's name.

One of us struggles with old confessions;
both, with pulling our mother out
from her un-absolved obsessions.

Dad stares sad like a foreigner;
speechless; un-translated.

Our parents' bond endures but gone
their vintage conversations –
ex-communicated.

The Glove Compartment

In the thrumming back of the car
my legs cramped by bagfuls of things
mother's stashed here for fear of swallowing,
I help her focus from the back seat,
her saner side, shut off with the powdered
glucose sweets in the glove compartment.
My eyes cast back to the bags at my feet.
She throws a panda-eyed stare
from the dark rear-view mirror.

Through the smudged windscreen my mock
composure shivers with leafless trees
twisting in the wind. Stark markers
for my probing on limits of time;
waning strength; deathly sky.
I'm lost in myself for grim minutes;
struggle to trace true bouts of substance
in outlines of thought-shaped clouds.

Mother Mouse

My tiny mother in her tiny kitchen
Rinsing the washing up –
A poem warped above the sink
Entitled *Don't Give Up*.

But Greeting Card wise pearls aside,
Sentiments tire now;
Thirty-five years she's survived
Each wrung-out wedding vow.

For better, for worse, for richer, for poorer,
A shine for bees-wing eyes –
A sud-filled cup for a moment's doubt –
Some sparkle for disguise.

She scurries around her mental wheel
Like an obsessing mouse,
Spins her chores like effortless confessions;
Swallows her sobs as she tidies the house.

Little Hells

Sun streaming in at seven 'o' clock
my fibrous nerves crumpling to
a pile of vampire bones in its light.
My refuge, pillbox dreams last night.
Life's lightning fork, indiscriminately,
charges me up with a pulsing shock.

Too stimulated by light, you'd think,
to appreciate it leisurely;
live afraid but inspired in anxiety;
primed dynamite – tensed, rhymed
for fear of letting go; cerebrally
greyed while young,
I flirt daily with the brink –

lead on my bed, morning's nerves revive me
pushing light in my head;
little Hells rise early.

Spiritual Gin

The lights are on in the Methodist Hall,
Shadows smudge through the frosted glass –
Come in ye thousands, come in ye all!
Bash out belief in a bible class.

The lights are on in the Methodist Hall,
The lights are on – is someone in?
It's cold outside in the chill of the Fall,
So come, tot up on spiritual gin.

It's grey outside and the windows glow
Like a giant cave troll's oblong eyes –
What goes on in there? Who's to know?
Better to doubt on the cold outside.

Those hall doors open to swallow some in
From dusty old ladies to faded old men
Sunday bested in berets and blazers –
They all wheeze in to praise their saviours.

Thursdays let in the down-and-outs
Dishing them out clean needle alms –
Visions of Jesus as they gouch;
Beatitudes like numbing psalms.

The lights are on in the Methadone Hall,
Opiums, masses, miracle cures free –
Come in ye thousands, come in ye all!
(This Church only seats 93).

Death in the Height of Summer

The day's dark in treacle-thick summer,
thunder claps applause for a mummer
of dark masks rumbling the sky. A smoke
to exorcise thought-ghosts. A poke
in tired eyes as reality bites –
beggars petting their Diamond Whites
in leathery hands with *Night of the Hunter*
knuckle tattoos, eyeball each punter
burping out from the pubs, with dim
pickled-egg pupils, gormless, unblinking,
dodging each-others' stares; the skies
blot more with inky cloud; light dyes.

Mind, turn-tabling away, too tired
to lift its stylus, unwind; so fired
with simmering intensities,
numbed in unrealities –
glimpsed down every passing side-street,
in pale faces I try not to greet,
in gaps between railings, fume-stained buildings,
is Death; in minutes' endings and beginnings,
in your difficult breath, your typical sigh,
Death hovers in the corner of the busy eye,
swells in the back of your mind, waiting
like a larvae saving up its sting.

Catching Sight of the Urban Fox

A bright May morning glows the supermarket bricks
Satsuma-orange, ambered by the sun
like blanching pages of light-warped paperbacks
in Oxfam's hothouse racks, two doors down but one.

A more debonair of down-and-outs,
a tramp who's used to tramping about,
so does in a mature, dignified manner,
pushes his supermarket trolley of belongings
– as if a golf bag in the absence of a caddie –
piled full with plastic bags, empty Coke bottles.

Comes to a philosophical halt
in nice patch of sun, meticulously tips
trolley on side, flaps out his coat-tails
like a pianist, then balletically sits.
Checks himself, nose twitching, ears a-flicker,
in his vast shaving mirror, the glass wall Waitrose
politely provided him and those of his sort
who need to keep check on their manicuring.

A very true gentleman, truest of all:
less incentive than most to keep himself tidy;
looks most refined, gentleman's tweed
cap positioned in perfect symmetry
with his clean-shaven face; thinning grey
straw-like hair neatly combed out
of all its irritating mites.

Only thing letting his apparel down
is his hole-torn rain-mac, a dust cover for
his more dapper fox-brown overcoat –
he looks like a fox, not crafty and devious
as Beatrix Potter's, but pointedly razor-
red of face (burst vessels from cold,

not booze; no soberer man has tramped
in such immaculately un-scuffed shoes);
alert, sharp, proud; most of all, free.

Spit of an eccentric country gentleman
unaccustomed to hustle-bustle bristling city life;
quite out-of-kilter in a Mad Hatter-ish way –
used to see them all the time, swinging on lamp posts
in Nineteen Seventies' Goring-By-Sea;
Mad Hatters we labelled them Carrollishly.

It's rare to get so close to an urban fox
scrimping in its stubbly native habitat,
licking mitten-paws to wipe its side-boards clean –
but he can't see me, doesn't sense my stare
depicting him in my bus-window hide,
invisible as a flea in his itching hair.

The Commuter's Last Stop

He stopped in his office eleven minutes late,
Face white as a plastic cup
Betraying twenty years wrung in shifts –

The only thing left in his life that went straight
Was his corporate noose and ironed-out cuffs.
His mind was an office without any lifts.

That day he was absent though he was sat there
Thumbing through paperwork, counting the clock,
Numbed to the plastic tap of the computer –

A blind typist deaf to his own dulled despair.
He swept up his desk; left early ad hoc –
Next day his train missed another commuter.

Lovers' Tiff

A romantic crisis breaks out like sweat
outside this steamed-up, greasy spoon pane –
I'm not concentrating on my chips and fried egg,
not seeing all the things in the street,
I'm looking straight through the passers by
as if they were daytime phantoms of life's
shadow dance round my sedentary thoughts.

I'm focused entirely on the face of the boy,
his pleading eyes trying to penetrate
the shaded emotions through his girlfriend's sunglasses,
tears slowly beading the rims of the lenses –
what's he trying to tell her as she trembles?
What's he struggling to express as he fingers
her tissue-clenched hands – mouths aren't moving –
whatever language they use it's not the tongue's.

Is he trying to let her down slowly while she
appeals to his conscience with troubling muteness?
Or is she turning her feelings from him
while he pleads silently with arresting eyes
for a second chance with her, which thus stirs a conflict
in her tangled feelings? Has he been disloyal?
Or is there an excuse in my following pun:
there's something more in this long pregnant pause?

As their bus pulls up, they slow-motion to it
and alight like lost love, and I know I'll not solve
the clues to their crisis, the time I've invested,
the thoughts I've commissioned to be interested,
my mind's curiosity stalled unrequited.

Life's Brief

Where you're going to there'll be no memory
to hamper you; no memory of who you were before;
it'll all be different – but I can't say how; not exactly;
but you'll comprehend it when you get there;
all will become less obscure like mists lifting.
You'll forget yourself and be something-else.
No more understanding for you, no more need
to understand; just being. At first you'll not think,
you'll not question, you'll not need to, any more
than a tree feels the need to fathom its own origins
or be aware of how many centuries it's lived –
only later on will you see that there's new
comprehending to do; new doubts to stall at.
Now you are nothing, but there you'll be something,
and will have to get used to purpose; a sense
of being known, yet lost; of being
innocent. They have a name for this state
and it is *life*.

Death's Breathtaking View

We clutch the threads that stitch our seamless lives
Immersed in glass routines like black shark eyes;
A sentence hanging over all our heads;
The grimace of a clock face offering
No other explanation but its ticking;
A faceless wall at the foot of our beds.

All we can be sure of is powerless doubt
And the door we came in will invite us out
To nonsensical oblivion or bliss;
Or a frozen limbo while turning the bend.
So we burn the candle at both ends.
In the meantime all we scrimp is this:

Faith in the soul, a light that leads us on
Through the dark to terrifying perfection –
Anything but nothing, to be lost in the night,
The pitch-white mist of a fog-bound sea,
The unthinkable smallness of eternity –
Anything but the turning off of lights.

Some seek solutions in the superstitious;
Gregarious others simply drink like fish
Clinking glasses they can't see through –
Salvation: saliva of the garrulous.
Perhaps the only sanity is madness
When comprehending death's breathtaking view.

Some take the plunge, pre-empt the sea;
In spite of being contradictory,
Cancel dark with dark. Obviate
The inevitable? Impossible; we know
All we've come to love one day has to go –
But what could be more morbid than to wait

Until the darkness swallows us? And yet
No sense in stubbing out lit cigarettes;
Best to leave just ashes for the ashtray;
To try and come to terms long in advance;
Stretch perception of deceptive distance;
Put off the problem for an umpteenth day.

Captain Parker's Trunk

Take a peep inside Captain Parker's trunk,
rummage through saffron-coloured photographs,
potter through old foreign objects,
bead photo-frames, bundles of First World War
scribbles indistinguishable from zareebas
of mummified spiders; finger
the bilious brass of grandfather's
medals, sneeze a salvager's sneeze
as further finds surface and dispersing dust settles –
it's an excavation with hands for trowels
but you may finger the bone-fine pipe,
the mouldy tobacco tin and khukuri knife.

Inside this lucky dip no toys,
but chipped regiments of broken model soldiers
buried in a cotton-wool cushioned box;
the same my father used to mummify
in tissues and hide in a drawer of the dresser
so my tampering fingers couldn't take off
the paint of their delectably coloured tunics
(now put away for good
with innocence and childhood
since I've grown up, lost interest in
pith helmets and Sudan campaigns).

Little remains of the trunk's namesake,
or his exploits; trips to distant shores;
salvage of Cleopatra's Needle
hauled from its bobbing grave;
his discoveries of Eskimos,
two of whom he chaperoned
back to Hull, housing them
in a shed in his back garden
(they pined away like stranded huskies
in their wooden igloo, lasting only
long enough to be frozen in a photo).

Little too survives of his Whaler son,
Captain Parker the second, save
a frame from which his sea-green eyes
stare at a bare landing wall;
vast canvas of black and amethyst waves
toiling beneath the ghost of his ship.

Grandfather paid tribute to his ancestor's
vessel by easing it into a bottle,
unfurling its paper sails with the pin-tug
of an intricate, miniature pulley system –
a marvel for father's childhood eyes
to *a fishy on a silver dishy.*

Most memories bundled in this trunk,
those of father's times: photographs
of his proud-faced father and kind-eyed mother,
and other dust-caked deceased ancestors
heaped deep in piles like shelves of the earth.

Father, family curator, tinkers
here to forget the present that pales
to the glow of the past; the sweet reassuring
smell of dust, relic, damp and nostalgia.

After something like a hundred years
sliding about on the creaking planks
of an oak-panelled cabin's floor,
Captain Parker's wooden trunk
is still in one piece and miraculously standing,
a tomb of mementoes, their sturdy refuge
from the dampness setting in on the walls by the landing.

The House of Sadness Past

After this fruitless time, the strife
of fifteen garbled cottage winters
dimmed in Trematon, I didn't
bid goodbye to the shrunken shack
bribed us to sojourn for time
unmarked by ageless slate West sky.

Chance missed to lay a lifetime
ghost to rest; leave behind
a difficult friend I fell out with
but stayed close to the bitter end;
a bond built on month-hours' foundations.

Too late to improvise goodbyes
in haunted stares, self-pity in rooms,
unrealised; plaster-pink walls,
unpainted; a damp-aired landing's
centre-reign, half-suggested...

*

I reassemble that tomb of stone
in its clump of weeds; hinge-creaked gate;
blue gloss door with Picksie latch;
derelict sunlight splintering where
twisted limbs of an apple tree
choked rotten spoils – soft crinkled skins
bruising to the touch: moth-thoughts,
hovering, tumbling numberless
as pebbled beds of crouching flowers
in those imprisoning mornings.

A cow-bell clopped to the overflow;
a carcass of glass spilt stinging nettles;
a cement-filled pebbledash well
pushed up shrubs of wishing petals.

Morbid, our umbrella word,
groping for a foothold in
laboured hours, weight of sadness
(there's the other word) as if
we lived our purgatory blurred in;
misting lives in suburbia.

Darkest nights I'd known;
moths, grotesquely outgrown;
hand-size spiders tapping on
peeling posters, clicking time
to the clock's taciturn ticks.

*

Bowed by the bent beam gazing over
warped books on the blistered sill
to the trampled sadness of our garden,
a tumble of nettle-tangled troubles
pouring from the house's mouth,
sculpting sorrows from sad panes –
a battered hat of buckling slates
trilbying its pockmarked face
of swollen stone: this house is ill.

Sold us as idyllic, white-washed,
it was a starker face: our own
little crumbled House of Usher
obscured by prouder abodes,
confiscated from the hamlet's view –
a disgraced sight set back from the road.

*

Stone-cool lounge, summer hung
thick outside, a fog of dream
struggling to wake the room,
bore in through the thought-sized crack
in the gloomy two-way pane;
the sooty cave of the fireplace,
focus of our shade – in winter,
of crackling logs' gooseberry-glow
spitting bilious flame.

Cuckoo-broken silence versed
with upstairs' floor-boards creaking
in an empty bedroom – a reassuring
ghost too shy to haunt us or
the panting scrape of earthly mother's
cobwebbed broom brushing the floor.

Some houses have souls, memories,
haunting them – this one had:
a sadness past remained, served
to feed ours with historic force.

I'll return, through the ghostly photo
of hollow windows' gormless glare –
an emptied relative's frozen stare;
grope up the slanting path into
its blossom-grey, cabbage-white
wintry circumstance, now time's
passed trace of us there...

Last of the Spray Carnations

Everything's through a haze today,
a nervy bleach, blurred photograph
exposed before developing
like a crippled Spartan baby;
a saffron-starched, sun-blanched album
family image, except it isn't
my family I mingle with, but a stunned
white drift of sun-paled faces probing
lichee-eyes into market bargains.

As if I looked at this bustling rock-pool
speculum of life through frosted glass
or a thick honey-coloured vase.

I trip on, lost to the fogged outside
of myself, part-deaf to the touting shouts
of the cod-eyed fishmonger, the sun-flushed
apple-shaped pink lady, lamb-shouldered
butcher with a scrag-end face, his
white coat reeking of bloody meat.

Everything, poetic and pathetic
at once, in a burst of cheap-side sunlight
scooping a pool on the scene.

Even the vivid spoils of the florists
appear pitiful: a cluster of pink
and white spray carnations,
green at the edges of thirsty petals
poking from a dripping bucket, a bunch
of scrunched-up tissues saturated
with tears of mustard sun.

The Gospels of Gordon Road

In parroting streets the Parkers lived
in an outburst of spilt belongings
by a pet shop perched on Gordon Road,
No. 31 – one score left to them;
muffled fluster of cockatoos
scratched the front-hall walls;
terrapins, tropical fish
splashed in a backyard aquarium
for a ghostly public, unforthcoming.

i. The Gospel According to Beryl

Obese-limbed Beryl, name the colour
of her bilious coat, avocados
she'd bleach with vinegar
supping on stories of Roaring Uganda,
kept a trove chockfull with spoils
of childhood paraphernalia:
a blanched pith helmet, *Elephants in Jinja*,
ebony carvings, tusks and tales
of a slate-eyed Scottish father
telegraphing the veldt
and ivory white goddess mother
biting poison from Boy on the veranda.

Composer of saccharine-pen letters
to all and sundry: from the star
of *The Flame Trees of Thika*
to Mrs Thatcher for being the first
menopausal PM – Iron Beryl,
fulsome as lukewarm Stout.

Her mantelpiece of miniatures:
a small glass Buddha with an ochre flower
in its bloated belly, 'if you rub his tummy
it'll bring good luck' she'd mutter through

the cryptic slit in her age-stitched skin,
with other superstitious snippets:
'pray to St. Anthony if you lose anything',
but he never recovered lost marbles.

Beryl believed in blonde baby Jesus,
cribs, clans, papacy, tooth fairies,
Clarabelle, Tinkerbelle, plaster saints
and table-salt superstitions – held
chair-ridden court cushioned in
upholstered throne, all swollen shins,
tortoise-shell glasses and netted hair.

ii. The Gospel According to Harold

Her trilby-humbled husband Harold
limped in slump of self-belief,
stick to buttress his step,
stocky North Londoner, Gunners supporter –
shuddered at jellied eels, bow bells,
'I'm not a cockney', he'd puff and profess,
proud of his old china tribe.

A rifle-butt buffeted his spirit
in a German camp, buffered him
with fits of temper, trembling limbs –
from Corporal Parker of the Buffs
to Private Struggle pensioned off
to the tyranny of landlords
and the mush of meals-on-wheels.

A legacy of long-term concussion:
de-mobbed prompt in '45;
assembling dolls' limbs in factories;
spell as shopkeeper bankrupted off
to last stop by Balfour Road.

In mouldering, damp-walled winters,
bereaved by his worshipped wife, coped
through a series of botched episodes:
Catholic conversion, gulps of pills,
macabre bed-time reunions
with his spiritual Beryl.

Harold went out like a flare in a trench,
refusing Last Rights in rabid-eyed rage,
leaving the Priest and the Pastor speechless
as the plastic Christ on his bedside table
he mistook for Mary as the beard had faded.

Four campaign medals, absent fifth
for a brave act screened off in gun-fog;
captured; tortured; frozen to snow
for escape attempts – never escaped
the stalking of the swastika's brand.
His prime predisposed to put him out in time:
namesake of his mythic brother,
killed 'spiking the guns' in the First,
smudged out with led like his last
pencilled scribbles blunt as his fate.

Harold rationed out his days,
guilt-inheritor, warped by self-blame
for the world's unanswerable blunders;
his prize: some debts and a pauper's grave.

iii. The Gospel According to Gordon

The Brighton Parkers played host to
a cadaverous bachelor, physsog threadbare
as his wicker sweater, also Gordon,
who lodged one ruptured flight beyond
obscure parameters of absent banisters
up a scupper of cuttlefish stairs.

A bachelor but for the merchant sea
he married, Gordon cut a skeletal shipmate
in his fisherman's cap and tweeds,
spruced on canine piss and bird seed.

Shut off in the trill and chirp of his
lemon-curd/sky-blue budgerigars
caging his company as a cancer-
growth his old dog Tony,
the gruff old lodger shrugged off thoughts
on gossip of souls and salvation:

'I don't believe in Heaven; nothing
after this 'far as I'm concerned;
best make the most of your pension'
he'd glibly comment if invited in
to give his shilling's worth of philosophical rent.

God scarpered from his dingy digs
in Gordon's head long ago to find
new lodgings in more malleable minds.

How odd him not believing in God,
I thought as a boy – my oblivion,
being alone – couldn't comprehend
his atheism, not knowing then
the dormant terms of my own.

iv. The Gospel of Gordon Road

We believe what we want to believe;
time buttresses us with splints of insight,
feeds us lies to starve doubts, to cope;
Gordon's tools, the mental present-ness of pets;
Beryl's, rent-book resurrection;
Harold's, ball-points on football pools.

Some make themselves their own God;
some spend their lives fishing for stars;
some endure all with a humble hat's doff;
some keep budgerigars.

Obverbs

Motto for the Mountaineer
If you try to reach the summit
You're likely to become it.

~

Age's Hill
Young Puritans of austere will
Grow cavalier past age's hill.

~

-isms
Capitalism spouts from city walls;
Socialism mutters in draughty halls.

~

Damp-Stain Angel
The vicar couldn't make it out at all:
a damp-stain angel on his chapel wall.

~

Fear of Blindness
Believing in God for a dread of death
is living in darkness for fear of blindness.

~

Death's Dress Rehearsal
Romans called asthma rehearsal for death;
life, summed up as a shortness of breath.

~

Sleepy Head
The man who looks like he hasn't slept well
has a face like a bed that's been slept in.

~

The Girl with the Dirty Hands
She held out her hands, begged for a fag
she got from the boy with no jobs in the bag.

~

Binds & Threads
From school to work there are common threads:
Clambering into winter out from warm beds.

~

Day & Night
The night can be what we want it to be
but the day shapes itself.

~

The Inevitable
Death is inevitable, but so is life –
Life is inevitable!

~

Failure's Finger Nails
Failure bites at its own fingernails;
Only fate's interpretation fails.

~

Class & Punishment
Grandfather took a horse-whip to father's arse
for asking him if he was working-class.

~

Sheds
We're apes with infinity in our heads;
we cut down trees and dream in sheds.

~

Graffiti
Graffiti is the spoor of dissidence;
claw marks of desperate residents.

~

Poetry Kills
I read the warning in my short breath:
Poetry's a slow and painful death.

~

The Inevitable II
The prospect of dying
almost drives me to trying.

~

While I Waited
What did you do today while you waited?
I read a bit, slept, then masturbated.

~

The Till-Girl
The Slavic till-girl with the harassed eyes
Scrapes a Co-Op opt out from blasted skies.

~

CV
The gap on my CV:
The time spent being me.

~

Curtain Call
If the world is a stage
That makes me a page.

[Note: Obverb = the author's coinage for obscure proverbs]

Dark Advice

If someone's about to kill themselves – distract them!
Asks what interests them, can't do any harm,
But if they really want to jump, let go of their arm:
At least that way they won't do it again.

Thing is, the only real danger's fear itself;
You might argue with this but you're wasting breath:
Suicide's the only way to kill off fear of death.
All best ways of soothing pain undermine your health.

The Buzzard

At a safe distance its stare exacted me
from its golden hay-stacked throne,
shining with all the bravura of the sun;
big-limbed king of Cornish ramble-lands,
stubble-fields and ragged hills –
talons size of manly hands;
on prehistoric scale
to my eyes cowering their ground on a hay-bale
by the cottage back window for retreat if needs be –
the Buzzard kept still, its feather-crown's plumage
ruffled by the breeze-brushed sway of its dynasty.
I was too cautious to take a closer look,
could only guess if its royal stare
translated the thought: which subject sits there?

The Sunday Poem

After I'd read the Sunday poem
I strolled out for the afternoon
to find some inspiration
leaving thick-lens-d middle-men
ink-thumbing through supplements,
completing crosswords while church-goers,
through cryptic sacraments, solved their
morbid ruminations
with breathless prayers
and sighs like silent skies.

Adam's Nib

It wasn't a woman tempted me
Into my fall, into my fall;
Just a piece of paper and a pen –
The imperfection of it all.

Signature like a Squashed Spider

You could have been any person,
You could have been any age,
Your signature could have been anyone's;
The proverbial spider squashed on a page.

Brain Smoker

If suddenly interested
he'd light up a Superking
cough up some knowledge
on this, that and everything;
only person I knew
who'd sigh with enthusiasm,
treat convert-sation
as a syllabic spasm –
think while he talked with visible ease;
at a slight interruption,
intellectually sneeze.

Meeting the Paint Eater

I saw a man with candles in his hat
trying to capture the moon –
as I passed by I said to him
'it's going to be supper time soon'.

His foggy eyes acknowledged my words:
he brushed his stubbled chin,
put some crumbling paint to his lips,
smiled, and started eating.

The Backpacker

She travelled to discover Truth;
Had photographic proof
Of how she found it by herself
Without the aid of parents' wealth
But through money she had saved –
Well yes, her job was quite well paid –
But she did it all off her own back:
Stashed the truth, a grain each day
In Kenya, Thailand and Bombay
On hash-stained postcards in her backpack.

RIP Lives

How many millions of Reginald Perrin's
Sigh at their ghosted pinstriped reflections
Stuck on the same cryptic clue every day:
Bolivian poet catches flu reading Proust
(Seven letters) – broad-sheet handkerchief
Crumpled in stale office-smelling suit-pocket;
Reflecting, regretting, returning to thoughts
Battening obsessions in clattering tracts,
Retracing tracks like commuter trains
Of reeking seats, rocking compartments
Conversationless as Surrey scenes
Smudging through the carriage-panes.

Gasping

Finish it up! Don't pour it down the sink
just because it's got too cold!
There's people **GASPING** for a cup of tea
on the other side of the world!

The Battle of Trafalgar Street

A laid-back lackadaisical day –
patisseries, espresso houses, busily
about their business – across the street
a tiff broke out like a summer sweat,
heated and burning-tyred: his bike
fell from under him with a punch –
people stopped as boot stamped face –
I froze on the spot as blood gushed out
from the football-head, flooding the street –
pummelling done, he belted off –
someone phoned for an ambulance.

Moleskin Man

A bedraggled stray slumped in dark tweeds
scribbling gibberish (?) in a rain-warped journal,
clutching a tennis ball, his latest find,
a curiosity purposing his tissue hands,
scuffed feet twisted in concentration
his whole world's belongings neatly dumped
in Sainsbury's bags – I can't touch him.
How can I help him? What can I do?
Bury him in my moleskin binds;
put his impotent life in a poem –
a paper scrapbook specimen –
then tip him out into other peoples' minds.

White Collar Rhyme

I found my purgatory in typist's pills –
salvation in secretarial skills –
glimpsed infinity in filing cabinets,
oblivion in invoices, audits,
spurred on to hanker for escape,
to rape
surplus paper supplies, pilfer
sheets to print my poems on –
a pinstripe poet out-of-kilter
with his misplaced gifts; ambitions
perpetually in delay
piling up in his in-tray.

Composing by Post

R.V.W. composed his letters
like his symphonies, green-sleeved he'd write
'My Bonny Boy' by formal post –

his feistier pen-friend thundered back
with striding Jupiters, signing
Your Future Inspiration, Holst.

The Old Pianos

I passed a shop full of old pianos
on the stave of a curb-lined street,
stared in on the old mahogany men
crouched round their stools in the shade,
baring their yellowing teeth, odd gaps
of ebony in-between – I lingered;
longed to brush white their un-fingered
gap-toothed ivories.

Per Mare Per Terrum

Sat on my father's marching knees
to *A Life on the Ocean Waves*,
he grins as salty sentiment staves
streams like Pacific seas;
cigarette smoke tousles and sails
out from his drumming hands;
whistling teeth biting his nails –
cymbal clash of the old Massed Bands

hisses to halt. Steady
on deck of landlocked lounge he stands,
swaying side to side as if still at sea.

Miss Clarke's Finishing School

Never write a poem with defective feet;
Never trust a poet whose eyebrows meet:
They're style's lycanthropus, hairy inside,
Celtic on the surface but English as the seaside;
Only rhyme if it's strictly necessary
Like at a poem's end to give more impact 'see;
No abstracts, just write about rrrrreal things:
Shells and Welsh cakes, wedding rings;
All manner of tangibles; amethyst, jade;
Salt breath of caves; tongue's dragon tails;
Woe-betide those who forget they're from Wales.

In The Laps of the Gods

I worship you because you give me love and warmth
with the magical touch of the strange white glow,
the smell of heat, wood-cool of ground
in summer, like outside, in the garden the air
blows our coats, fanning our stifled fur –
and the scent of the out: the leaf, the earth,
the language of dirt-tracks, the freedom, space;
the clinging scent of your hand as it strokes my hair
reassuring me with its familiar smell
when I grow lame and can't get around,
out of LOVE for me you'll put me down.

The Guilty Building

The eyes of the windows were guilty, shut
above the baroque walls of the bank,
shadow hovered behind their gaze,
the mouth of the polished Georgian door
closed mutely on the street – no sound
issued from the impartial building,
or did but wasn't detectable for
the whispers of shoed feet on the ground.

A Photo of Vaughan Williams

Clouded, the colour of the composer's eyes
for the photos in black, white and greys –
the misty grey of wistful Wilfred's parted
in the centre stare. Pipe, woodbine,
props to compliment enigma – smoulder
stinging foggy sepia pupils - there's
a face for inspiration, the flash of an artist
about it, despite the battledress, no doubt
who snapped it up had that intention.
Can the camera capture the soul?
Can it photograph the God in us?

Don't Envy the Empty Sun

Ponders the park, mustard of leaves
canopy lovers from pelting solitude –
no self-imposed ice-queen cooped up by choice
in a vanity palace, more Sleeping Duty
who never quite woke up despite pills
and acupuncture to stimulate
time-numbed nerves, lift her from
the mine-shaft of sadness before it caved in.
Shouldn't envy their empty sun. Droll
pond life doesn't ponder its reflections.
Only those mind-incarcerated like her
in protracted correspondence with the soul.

The Poet Tree

We left to make home in a shell of stone,
garden left to ramble overgrown
making itself notoriously known,
overblown, wouldn't be mown,
as a mop of unruly hair won't stand a comb.

All dandelions and weeds; a sun-starved tree
couldn't bear fruits – we had to show it
by planting another in its shaded view.

But in time a home had grown;
daffodils twinkled; the shy, leafless tree
blossomed into a poet.

The Blackboard

My first glimpse of oblivion:
the school blackboard, to me then
my life seemed like one scrape of chalk
smudging into the dark.

Innocence Twisted

Too soon some said he spoke
with a sour taste,
and saw how innocence
twisted on his face.

Chasing Shadows

Tipsy with nostalgia we
miss those times of Time's slower pass
when we were children trying to chase
our shadows on the grass.

Spilt Milk

Sometimes I think I'm just soul and mind,
A spirit without a jacket of skin,
No flesh and bones, just pockets of air;
A milk-filled statue of porcelain.

Intrusive Thoughts

Outnumbered by invisible bullies
punching at my equilibrium,
bruising with intrusive thoughts,
I despaired (can't think of a better word)
as I followed the other boys down to
the muddy pitch: scared of stopping
loving my father, though impossible,
it tormented me for frozen moments;
I panicked; couldn't figure it:
numbed by the obsessive buzz
of fear-bees bumping about my head.

The Drive

Either to be a premature dread-end
or terrible beginning, my thoughts juddered in
my darkening humid mind overcastting
with summer storm cloud maundering
from the blind east; tight eyes straining
to fathom detail of relentless hedgerows
cramping our car on narrow lanes
horribly idyllic in stretch – rain splattered
in harassing spits drumming the bonnet,
obsessing a web of drops on the windscreen –
the wipers screeched *Can't Cope! Can't Cope!*

Orange & White

High above Granada's green fountains
and orange tree vistas, the mountains
smudge through the mists of summer.
The sawdust earth is a bull-ring colour.
A moth cavorts in the sun-blanched grass;
A dark thought hovers past.
Houses below slabbed like ice-cream
Wafered with roofs of orange sheen;
Spanish vanilla melting in the glow
of the incessant sun – *naranja y blanco.*

Beatitudes

Today, everything's resolved: the man
with the rainy Sunday face has found
a smile's an inspiring beam of light
in his outlook; the senile lager-breathing
dragon of withered scales, forced to forgo
his habit for the day, is the better for it:
sober and brave; the two middle-aged
friends have let bygones be for a change;
the doubting housewife's found her faith,
vacuuming behind the chairs.

Five Minute Infinity

In the space of five minutes I held you, said,
half to myself, half to you, 'how did I
deserve you?', thought only of my fear
of dying, tried convincing you
of the soul while I wasn't convinced myself;
and you said you'd no fear of death only
of lingering suffering (that atheist chestnut)
– but why don't atheists fear death
when they're more certain of it?

Who fears death needs the crutch of faith;
who fears pain needs the crutch of death.

In The Mist

Church bells' chime in pea-soup September,
sirens of sea-gulls dispersed by their peals...

mist shimmers in from the hills
smudging its presence on city mills...

invisibly drifts like spirits by
trees crucified against the sky...

the church bells' stop chiming...
lives chime by...

Death Wears a Homburg

With some pills and booze he took off his shoes,
scribbled a note 'stead of learning his lines;
in a sedated haze, coined his last phrase:
things just seemed to go wrong too many times.

A sad washed-up clown with a long dog-jowl frown
his life seemed a mess like the sheets on his bed,
so with one final sigh and no look in his eye,
he put his life down like a book half-read.

Identifying Tim

He took his life too seriously.

Would he have been so serious now
if he'd had a united identity –
not talking, stopping, listening, brow
creased in concentrated scrutiny
of private voices – would he now
be tucked up early in eternity?

He took his life too suddenly.

The Cripple

See his skin distemper
To laburnum-green –
His eyes dart like a dog's
That cannot tell its dream.

The Brain of God

I used to wonder if the earth
was our creator's cerebrum,
and the universe, the space
inside His cranium.

Flowers in the Vase

Suddenly a fire stoked up inside me –
It was something someone said.
I thought the flowers were in the vase
But they were still in the flower bed.

Something someone said – shhh –
Or the sound of the fire fizzling out in water,
The dirty water which, hissing, said:
The flowers in the vase are dead.

Mist

Missed
while here
like mist
in rain;
once gone
forgotten
in all
but name.

Cradle to Grave

We all fall from water
and slide into flames
to the funeral organ's
bellow and wheeze –
start out with birthmarks,
end up with carved names –
from seeds grow to weeds
that cradle our graves.

Alan Morrison

Grandma's Ingredients

I discovered at a tender eleven
Grandma was made of buttons,
Brooches, rings and leather watch-straps,
Gift-wrapped in cellophane for heaven.

Oblivions

The sun, the sky, the land, the sea –
it's all been a bit too much for me.

To smell, to taste, to touch, to see,
to think, to feel, to love, to be –
it's all been a bit too much for me.

By finding the oblivion in me
and the oblivion in you, might be
the end to my sensitivity -

but the need to belong, to be free -
it's all been a bit too much for me.

Infinite Things

I can't enjoy anything that must end;
Infinite thoughts and feelings with limit;
Mortality's labyrinth trails bend on bend
But leads only to what is in it.

Timétations

i. The Bin of Time

Browbeaten by routine's tyranny
ravages of wasted time
cuttlefish your luminous brow,
sleeping-pill white, marble eyes:
pay with daytime drowsiness
for nocturnal sedated bliss
numbing your mind, cushioning thoughts:
well-punched pillows supportable for once.

ii. Time Bites

Hours hover, mothballing minutes
in static dust-clots, stick in the throat
as pills without enough water
to dissolve to flakes; time,
the irritable master it is, spits ticks
of rhetoric in gusts of stale breath
humming from a scoured tongue –
time bites like sharp radish,
a taste relished by the toothsome
while wisdom mints it out with gum.

iii. Closing Time

In cigarette-mist of a smoke-filled pub
he sat hand on head, wrist on chin,
'I'm trying to keep my brains in', he said.

Tears of snakebite streaming down
in lagered trace, misty eyes
disguised his tears, wasn't the place –

frozen, beered up, numbly waiting
for another round, dreading last orders
beckoning through tobacco smog –
could see his life half full, half empty,
clinging to his pint till closing time.

iv. White

Luminous cuttlefish sky stares pearly eye,
vast blank page, junket white winter sun
cocking a snook through parted clouds;
ghostly pale agoraphobic pate
parted by net-curtains' communion veil;
page of skin clinging, clinging;
sockets for eyes; cod-fish white glinting,
grinding nerves to powder, grinding
like the famished teeth of time.

v. Out of Clock Time

The soul knows no limits – I sense
this in my silent times – ticking
digits count only bodily lives –
but the soul, the self, the spirit lives in
its own domain outside clock-time –
ghosts, some think, cross to our side,
sometimes – a bit like obsessives popping
back to check they've remembered everything:
the gas; the keys; watering of ashtrays;
or simply to remember to collect what they
forgot to the plodding tock of days.

vi. Old Father Time

Time is a bitter, morbid old man
who can't hear what you're saying
or just can't understand.

vii. Time Anxiety

Life without the anxiety of Time
Might prop us up in our tripping prime;
If we could cut down clocks like trees
We'd put the branches at their ease.

vii. The Clock That Forgot the Time

What Time is it? asked the clock who'd forgot it.
Well if you don't know, how should I? replied
The Memory that couldn't remember. *What's the Time?*
Piped the poor Clock once again, then sighed.
That's like asking. . . said the Memory – . . .*no, I forget it.*
I would have asked Death, said the Clock, *but he's died,*
And Life's far too busy regretting it.

ix. Little Father Time

Pallid offspring of future-minded parents,
torn too soon from nursery rhymes
thrown into dingy itinerancy
of rented tenements, uncertain tenancy,
a rag doll dragged through Christminster streets
by the scruff of the cockerel's neck,
son of two fugitives in limited times,
protector of wind-bitten little siblings,

windfall babies, daren't rock-a-by
them lest crimped cradles fall –
pale twisted innocent, twisted by love,
hair sweat-greased from compassion's high fever,
all the world's troubles rub his marble brow
as if to polish off all infant fortitude –
Is there nothing to do? Is there nothing to do?
'Nothing' sounds out like a terrible blow
to his callow, cramped conscience, perilously raw;
nothing to do but sacrifice the lambs
then atone with immature martyrdom –
hung by shoe-straps, hands pillow-soft,
a crime of compassion in a child's despair;
a scribbled note slid under stool-wedged door:
becos we are too menny. How many more?

The Need to Dream Forever

I remember I was barely fed,
Eleven or twelve, in a freezing bed
Damp with doubts, wanting outs,
Drift off and dream forever...
Thought I wanted to be dead –
'Go to sleep', dad said.

Poem on Empty

Sat on the rag-and-bone sofa smoking
a singed dog-end in my ripped pyjamas,
staring at mug-stains on the lamp-lit table,
I said to my father, suppressing the groan
of my empty stomach, 'just to think
no one will ever know of this...'

The Haunted Ghosts

A face peered through the two-way window
of our shadow-cottage; squinting in
with sun-shade hand, he shook back as
the dogs claw-scraped up to the ledge,
barking ferociously as Cerberus
at the gates of Hades; I, Orpheus
with my shrinking father quickly stirred
as if discovered in a rustic squat
(the limbo we shades haunted) –
'I'm sorry' called the trespasser
through the starved glass gingerly
retreating, 'I didn't think this house
was inhabited' – and nor did we.

The Coin Foragers

In darkling days of testing means
we found distraction in playing games;
one comprised four players,
rules always the same:
each foraged for mouldy copper tokens
hidden in the scrimping room,
collecting as many as they could find.

Some stuffed in the glooms and crumbs
of the settee's cushions; some
stashed in the clutter of the kitchen dresser.
The winner: first to disinfect their treasure.

The Stain

           you can't wash out
no matter what powders you use;
the bitter taste you can't rinse from your mouth
with sap from a toothpaste tube;
the tactless smell you just can't shift
despite your effort trying;
the pasty stain your face is stuck with
that can't be changed by dyeing.

Dead Reminder

Thought-shelves list through lack of means:

book-binds losing stick split their seams,
prop each other up, nodding down-and-outs,
no one caring what they blurt about.

Tales aren't tall as bills, poems don't pay rent.
Pencils crack their points in tensing hands.

Tie a noose with plastic rubber bands:
find a dummy bouncing like his cheques.

Heirlooms

Starting from scratch, a clean slate, no class
Dismantling the furniture of the past –
I'd take a kit of tools straight away to this task
But sadly some furniture is built to last.

MIGHT

Why did some of us come to believe
The Left is in the right
When it has a massive clumsy body
And wings too small for flight?

Missing Ism

Dowdy tabby
tatty but distinctive,
answers to 'Socialism'.

Death of a Socialist

'It's easy to be a socialist when you've only yourself to think about'
muttered the veteran gargoyle of the left with bitter irony,
features crumpled as a rolled up *Morning Star*, front page
scanned, contents skipped by the masses it calls to arms
'– having kids taught me how honour has to scrape and bow
 for the sake of love. No greater cause. Socialism knows
no get-out-clause: Marx, like Christ, asks us to
sacrifice private interests for the public good;
turn our little families into big commun-
-ities. Well if everyone else did,
then I would.'

Riddle of the Sphinx

Riddle
What creature goes on four legs in the morning;
Two during the day;
And three in the evening?

Solution
The worker who begs on all fours for a job;
Gets up on two to paw for his pay;
Then limps with a stick when forced into leaving.

Aneurin

He was every Welsh housewife's hero,
every miner's pride;
all their children cherished his stories
tingling by the fireside –
how Kier Hardie's ghost showed him
in the pit a glimpse of Heaven
in the minds of men, *And you,* he said,
will fight to build it, Aneurin Bevan.

The Dark and Keir Hardie

Coal-blind Hardie learnt to see,
At least metaphorically,
As his stinking fish* lit up the way
To a dazzling Socialist day -
The autodidact stood to be
First Member in the menagerie
Of all things Parliamentary;
Formed a workers' party –
Tea-sipping Fabians admired his free
Messianic zeal but in his shabby tweeds,
Found him altogether unsightly.

* [Note: some miners used to use rotten fish, which glowed in the dark, to light their way in the pits]

The Sound of Eating

My great grandfather, a Fabian,
never skipped a single meeting
to discuss best ways of feeding
empty bellies of the down-at-heel.

(Privately he ate his meals
in his study, apart from his kin:
he couldn't stand the sound
of other people eating.)

Victuals

i. Transubstantiation

First Communion: First Sin:
Forgot, God, forgot to go Confession:
No Absolution: maybe Damnation?
Incensed Him in initiation.

I open to receive His Body nonetheless,
Innocent to my callow sin's trespass.

They'd said the bread, unleavened,
Would taste a bit like Heaven:
Had my taste-buds given up at seven?

Confusion at the flavour of the Saviour:
It doesn't taste of anything.

ii. Holy Roofs

The roof of the church
caked in tasteless Salvation
like the roof of the mouth
at Holy Communion.

iii. Absence of Butterflies

I recall as an altar boy watching the priest
breaking the unleavened bread,
placing one half in my hand which I placed
on my tongue where it transubstantiated;

now, as an adult, my doctor prescribes
a pill for my thoughts; nightly I break
a little white sleeping pill to attain

peace of mind and body; to slake
pins and needles of my nerves; numb
my stomach's downhill roll, steep rise –
but when I wake, like doubt from faith,
I feel the absence of butterflies...

The Fade

Life's a string of mistakes –
the best ones, those
we don't know we've made.

Love's a dying high –
a favourite song
going into the fade.

The Linger of Yearning

I'm left the shadow of your memory,
a linger of yearning to know
if there was no other what light you'd throw
on the room in your cramped heart for me?

Reversing Charges

Undressing her speeches, making love to her
over the phone while she
breaches the silence by spilling her change
and sending some sighs back to me –
the reversing of charges adds up passion's largesse
and mad sense of urgency.

The Commuter Belt

Reflections smudge on carriage-glass,
Darken to the howl of an underpass,
Screech of a fast concrete
Monster with stout stone feet
Planted either side of the snarling track.
Elephant thoughts lurch back
Intrusive trunks to hose the moment
With sprinkles of obsession: cogent
Trains of thought are stalling now;
Brass-horns signal the blousing plough
Of a steam engine's crutching ghost
Chuffing its pistons, pitching the post,
Summoned, a hunter of ivory
By trumpeting elephants – predatory
Ruminations distemper the tongue
With acid-stabbing, thought-bubble gum;
Invade the mouth, fleshy fumble,
Stinging sweet in tongue-and-tumble,
Swelling to bursting point balloon –
A stark, pulsating, light-bulb moon –
Deflated by the prick of a star
Hisses serpentine sighs of sin, ssssaaah!
Singling you out as guilty because
Someone has to give shape to a cross.

*

Hunter, hunted? No more sure
Than a profligate of expenditure,
A gambler of chicken and egg,
A beggar of how best he can beg –
An obsessor who seldom remembers
His Augusts, only Decembers,
Forgets how he came to his vocation,
When, at what platform location;
All but the in-growing image

Expanding brain muscles with spinach
Of rumination; the terrible picture
Pre-Raphaelite in vivid tincture,
Nightmarishly lurid, grotesque
In feverish colour – no sketch
But a study in detail on detail
Glossed over, re-coated for retail
To parade on taut hangers to browse
Over strait-jacket to blouse.

*

A blowzy commuter with infinite ticket
Has counted each twig in the thicket
Blurred between Bognor and Havant;
Possesses an obsessive talent
Obscure, not totally certain
It's lifted its long dusting curtain –
And what of his spirit, its scraping by
Halfway between the trees and the sky,
Burnt to a cinder in ashtrays of scrub,
Singeing the end of a butt you can't stub
Out, though you twist it to squeak its last
Ember, it burns on igniting the past,
Till you're grateful for stops at bland platforms:
Mundanity massages mind-storms,
Brushes cobwebs of doubt, frees the crane-fly
From spiders of worry spinning you high,
But this spell of bliss is too brief
Like lapsing from faith to belief,
Depending on what you're believing
Can be paralysing/relieving –
But Belief only limbers a bit of the way;
Doubt's sun pours down in the panic of day.

*

Beads of sweat dripple down, rivulets
Of irrational currents, face reflects
Shimmering in hazy shallows of the glass –
Scrappy escarpments, allotments pass:
Cabbage patches stand on parade
For wheelbarrow-men to inspect from the shade
Of sheds; unsettling; the rut of the line
Scratches tracks for the trillionth time
But there's safety in whooshes and clatters,
Newspaper Hares and Sane Hatters,
Crumple of supplement, cling-filmed eyes
Frozen east as the stone crow flies –
Sardined in seats of dark tartan
Designed by meticulous Spartan,
Passengers parley eyes with scuffed shoes
Upturned dung-beetles that hum where they choose
Fuming compartments with odours as stale
As passage of time on the dragging of rail.

*

Time's no great Healer, Time's a slow burner,
And this particular victim, slow learner:
A mental escape artist who can't escape,
Long lost his knack, long out of shape,
Still handcuffed by attempts to resist
So doubts pursue, obsessions persist,
A humming swarm bumping in his mind
Stumbling indefinitely behind
Every feeling, impulse, implosion,
Every moment's mind-blowing explosion
Shooting splinters of shrapnel throughout
Each labyrinthine turning of doubt,
Coursing through tunnels of thought
Ploughing deep furrows, a demon dreadnought
Cruising to freak waves, crashing the surf
Muscling through, sucking its girth,
Chugging on dumb to the end of the track –

It's prize: not having to trundle back.

*

But the commuter belt loops on and on
An unrelenting, morbid song
Locked on track to a stalemate station
Departs before arrival – destination
Eludes its trick-snaking trickle through
Countryside of continuous view,
Changeless panoramas: paeans
To thoughts mutating in their trains...

Sui Oblitus Commodi

I came to know my father's parents
through dandelion recollections
scattered in their Crematorium.

Recognised John from a photo:
hook nose cushioned by strict moustache;
listened intensely to his crisp voice,
faint but distinctive,
slicing through hissing speakers
interspersed by clattering crockery
courtesy of his second wife's porcelain hands:

saintly Lily, preserved in sepia
snapshot from Heaven's after-flash;
those soft grey eyes epitomize
sui oblitus commodi –
she lived a secret in their stark house at Rock;
father often found her knelt, a grounded angel,
scrubbing the floor, chained to chores
as a suffragette to railings:

she fluttered into strictness' ether;
groomed in contradiction by
a Fabian father who dined alone
throwing Baptist scraps at the poor;
inherited his sentiments
(and sensitive stomach)
sweeping her Socialism
under a patch of carpet.

My country right or wrong rang hollow
from the pipe-propped mouth of her patriotic husband,
a splinter of rhetoric lodged in him
like a papery Kipling battle scar;
no stomach for Sassoon as he

had none for his son's *guts-ache* music,
Walton/R.V.W./Holst.

She: no stomach for selfishness
in her domestic soldiering;
strain of countryside seclusion
wrung her threadbare fibre dry,
manacled in phantasms;

her nerves took on the jolting force
of housebound bomb-shock (triggered by
doodlebugs she'd body-sheltered
her son from back in wartime Windsor);
no outbursts, just shattering silence,
obsessions cobwebbed about the morbid
cottage of her thoughts;

'My face has gone' she'd say in horror
before the mirror, 'I can't see it,'
or proclaim she'd lost her nose –
abstraction's Harpies plaguing her
with fears of blindness, formless impulse
throwing her from cliff edges
of thought, fed off her dread of dying,
her frightened love of life.

She laboured on to know one grandson,
witness the birth of a second, held him
in her thin, bone china arms,
hushabying under thundering breath.

Perhaps a little of the light in her
brushed off on me before it passed:

I share her sensitivities,
phobias, foibles, beliefs,
yet these in-grew as I grew out

from childhood's idolising of
her husband's disinterred ideas:
subordination of the self
for the nation – in that sense
a different ideal still deserving
sui oblitus commodi.

---
*forgetful of one's own interests

Only Rosie Smokes

All rickety wood desks and chairs,
Garish matt-lemon pimply walls;
Unlit corridors that trail to stairs
Where a ghostly hum summons from the hall:
The irritable lift, grumbling empty –
Deep in this labyrinth of gingery glimpses
Into hobbit-offices shut off like thoughts
On problems that haven't solutions
Bides faded, buck-toothed Rosie wrinkled
As a walnut, sole heir to the privilege
Of lighting up at work, poised with
Perpetual Silk Cut as she hunches,
Screwing her eyes at faceless audits
In the swirling vapours of her vice
Like Lewis Carroll's Caterpillar.
Fogs of rank fag-smoke for six hours
Percolate with the filtered coffee
Like the scent of hash in a Kashmir arcade.

The Renewers

i.

There's a reverence to a library,
hint of the Catholic sanctuary
for the skint, culture-hungry public
to life's open polytechnic
who can only afford to borrow words.

In monastic shade, off a Protestant street,
nun-like librarians abide by silences
vowed on Job Centre referral forms.

Stamping issues, re-shelving returns
in alphabetical sacristies;
renewing sinners through confessions,
some long overdue.

Battered books, bindings splitting,
hard-back, soft-back, dust-jacket souls
issued, renewed, returned, absolved.

ii.

Lovers of words, cerebral lepers
shiver in jackets outside the library
queuing in bookish solipsist politeness
for mind-alms to be meted out,
nourish their souls and intellects
with recycled scraps of escape.

One, old and faded of cover, coughs
with grind of tired lung, looks
a well-seasoned apple-scamp
through dim windows at greengage books,
thirsting their ripeness to renew.

10'o'clock gives twitching introduction
so in the letter-lusting file
for their cud of fact or fiction.

Jerome's Last Judgement
A Tribute to Jerome Moross, composer (1913-1983)

Adam and Eve on horseback
Galloping roughshod down through the canyons
Ricocheting contrapuntal brass,
Strident strings, trumpeting stampede –
Giddy-up sin in the Valley of Gwangi
Vine leaves for saddles, apple-stalk stirrups
Steering their stallions onto the climax
Of cymbal-clashing Culpa Felix –
What better crescendo for the Fall of Mankind;
Why not rouse the spirit, shiver the spine
Into new territories: *Eden – The Western.*
Temptation's volleys career until sundown
In Eden's Paradise Chaparral –
'This Garden ain't big enough for both of us, Satan!'
The Cowboy composer breaks through the corral
Of symphonic mores, gifts us a vision
Of God just a bit like Charlton Heston,
Lassoing Creation from under a Stetson.

Three Scores & Tea

Elfin Stevie, flame-haired naïf,
frocks and socks at forty-odd,
stamping her iambic feet,
casting spells to filibuster Time
who shrugs Its shoulders, admits defeat,
lets her off all-tainting certainty
blanching the couch in the bay window glare.

Death comes even to suburbia.
Aspidistras wilt like shadow spinsters.
Doily wills curbed by window-sills
turn in on themselves for three scores and tea
in Aunt Lion's best-china-rattling tray –
one lump or two to spirit her away.

Poor jilted Freddy, cup-sipping pity,
might have patched one flesh together
had she pinched her nose,
held her breath
but as wife she'd very little to offer
but bitter wit and junket;
an infantile infatuation with Death;
besides, her typist's fingertips
were only prone to wander keys.

Shelf-in Stevie, faded old maid,
her life, one long settee sit-in
on timeless catnapper, cigarette-
-singe verses to stimulate her mind
deeply morbid in the thundery gloom
of static parlour, crochet dull –
she'd have believed in God had He
not been a vengeful, damning one
but she could never reconcile
the Christian Doctrine of Eternal Hull.

Martin Goth

Martin, Martin, Martin, I remember when
You erupted in the night shelter threatening
To heed the voices, spectral tempters,
The invisible tormentor you pointed to
Over my sentient shoulders
When I spoke with you about those old coins
You collected – your limbered limbs
Brimming with adrenalin from one hundred press ups
A sweat-stench humming like an aura
Of possession about your gangly body –
'I am not insane, there's nothing wrong with me'
You asserted with a dark and stabbing stare,
Livid to why the 'mental health team' came
To the hostel to check on you – 'If you're quite sane,'
I started with untypical Odyssean guile,
'Then why are you so scared of seeing them?'
Your aggression subsided: 'Ok then', you said
And, fooling for my logic trick, tripped in to see them.

Well Martin, it seemed you convinced them
Of your 'stability', for the time being;
That or your adamant refusal to take
A hospital free trial or medication
Stalled them in facilitating your salvation.

I recall your obsessive vegetarianism:
You suspected meat harboured alien properties
Poised to contaminate you with mind-altering extracts –
That time I picked the meat bits out
Of your dish of rice, you still detected
The presence of animal chemicals
But you weren't in possession of all the fats.

I cast a dark eye back to your
Monochrome presence, long gothic-black

Man with beret displays deft marksmanship
with *porrón*: thread of red resuscitates flagging,
parched-mouthed Spaniard, stubble ruby-clagging.

3.
The Diggers, Keir Hardie and George Bernard Shaw
would have been in their elements in Barcelona:
no classes, differences, privileges here,
no profits, no tips for waiters or bootblacks,
a city collectivised, transport for all
in red and black taxis and trams on the Ramblas;
formalities, titles, traditional greetings
all levelled: *Senor, Don, usted* transposed
into *Comrade* and *thou*, even *buenos días*
replaced with *salud!* Now cats look at kings
straight in the eyes and square in the face,
Socialism in action – so much for the Church
of Spain, its capitalist altars: a trace
of deep-veined anarchy clots the character
of this Roman Catholic, Agnostic race.

4.
Green dreams of dust-jacket crusades
to battlefields of excrement and jagged tins,
bullet-rattled hills, birdless valleys,
villages sprawled like scattered dice,
crinkled hillsides like elephant hides
looming cold daunting – insect figures
shivering round flags, hugging flames
of pilfered Church candles they strike their lights by,
coughs for confessions in sandbag pews,
mortars sacred as plaster Madonnas
too precious to touch or use –
stagnation on the Aragón front;
heated exchanges of smoke-breathed views.

5.
The shabby freedom of a nation defended
by ragged children with sticks; greyed youth
greasing corroding scrap-iron rifles
with olive oil – *keep your powder dry*
cried Oliver Cromwell in a greener war,
now black and sea-green is black and blood-red
knotted in scarves round sticking necks
the colour of quail's eggs.
Don't tap the butt on the limestone ground!
Blunderbusses go off indiscriminately,
only guns are non-partisan here
along with the shakes and pneumonia –
not forgetting 'impartial' bombs that take out
the thrower as well as the target,
killing two stones with one bird.

A fag for a bomb worth throwing; a flag
for a trusty rifle; a cause for a clause
worth fighting for in this war against virus,
impasse against men; conflict postponed
for too distant pitching of camps and dug-outs
on honeycombed hillsides; sand-martins' nests.
The cracking of bullets on Fascist machine guns:
nuts hitting stones. These freezing soldiers
ache for battles and cigarettes
but night and the Jesuit return empty-handed.

6.
Shouting instead of shooting:
verbal bombs bounce from camp to camp;
starved cats have fasted for shouting duty
so hours of vocal volleys follow fuelled
on lack of *tabaco*, gut-rumpus of hunger
and spirits that scavenge glimpses of hope

on blue-smudged horizons, sights thrown amok
like a scamper of tramps scrimping fag-ends,
itching in lousy hair-shirts and goat-skins,
fleas hopping ship to and fro.
Futile mascots abound: a frozen
Moor in No-Man's-Land.
What gullible bribe brought him in the service
of Christians and Catholics? Should have fought
with us: raiders of gold-spoilt Churches;
we modern Roundheads; recusant hunters;
goosy ganders with highfaluting passwords
chiselling off Heavens from the headstones,
turning God's bullet-pocked Houses
into sanctuaries for smashed furniture and excrement.

7.
Casualties, the inevitable price of clashes;
competing with bombs, sirens caterwaul
from streams of juddering ambulances
that rescue the wounded, jolt them into corpses.
Sadly not as regular as faeces that spoors
in rank latrines, gifting rafts for rats,
is the infrequent trickle of Fascist deserters
inspired by catalysts of sparring polemic
ricocheting like cartridges through No-Tramp's Land:
Viva el POUM – Fascistas maricones! and so on –
arguments, like the spit of bullets, seem never-ending.
Damp trenches cause a passion for warm baths and clean sheets.
Polemic warms the farm house: heated politics
debated in freezing, rat-infested dug-outs
sandbags for soap boxes, bullets for ballots,
ideology in action on inactive battlefields
of barbed-wire –isms, shell-splintered -wings;
pens dipped in blood; bayonets dripping ink.

8.
The battle-scene: a war-torn bed chamber
exposed to skies for a roof scooped by a bomb:
bedsteads for barricades; bed-pan latrines
filling with yellow water from urinating rains,
rats large as cats splashing in them like otters –
hardly the picturesque brocade crocheted by
fevered imaginings in rapt English bed-sheets
before the pan was spilt; and barely picaresque:
the only rogues here are rats and grenade-pins
and Catalan cats staring out Spanish kings –
who doesn't know the way to a monarch's heart
is through explosives? Cue Guido Fawkes,
the Catholics' last coup with grit and gunpowder
to blow down Parliament's pack of cards,
towers of matchsticks and ratified tricks.

Who will oust out this brute Franco?
The folk songs of Lorca? The buzz of de Falla's
swarming *El Amor Brujo?*
Not strums of flamenco, stamping fandango,
choreographed toreadors' pugilist ballet
in blood-coloured dust of the bull rings.

9.
On the Aragón front flares clash with the flash
of clean bayonets, white armlets and gritted teeth,
or the whites of the eyes of terrified sheep
herded by bullets in the still lunar darkness
black as liquorish-root cigarettes –
thanks to Franco's annexed Canary plantations –
on grounds pockmarked with shell holes like
the cratered moon. What contrast by day:
faces stained by white ferocious suns,
windburnt; sunbeaten. Gnarled-faced Andaluces
bask in anarchy of classless ranks,
prized for their deftness at tucking in ends
of cigarettes shovelled with brittle tobacco.

10.
On a chattering train anís-totting
leather-faced peasants reflect the drab palette
of conscripted cats' coarse brown and khaki
who naturally care only for a fresh packet
of fags: a day's wage for philanthropy
at ten pesetas, price of altruism
along with rice-leavened bread, consistency
of communion wafers; bread like putty;
screaming trams and milkless tea;
scourge of olive oil; cigarette famine;
pounding stomachs in tortuous streets.

11.
¡Hola otra vez Barcelona! The lights of this city
of labyrinthine intrigue pinched out like candles
in Church-like dark cast by Tibidabo,
hill from which el Diablo showed
Christ the countries of the Earth – Franco's
shadow obscures truth, inspires
Communist plots, Valencian papers
flaming with Fascism – the Fascist plot:
Impeach the POUM – suppress the lot!
Adios Maurín, la Confederación Nacional
de Trabajo, *La Batalla's* championing
of the Friends of Durruti. Nín disappears
like invisible ink while libellous blots
of lily-white foreign newspapers stain
red permanent slander on hearts and minds
of lamb; give the view of the Balaclava hill
through safe sights of picnicking opera glasses.

We are called Fascists behind our backs
and behind our fronts – *No hay tabaco –*
Quiroga, Barrio, Giral – Bilbao.
Communist policies of pin-pricks pummels

subtly away at the honour of the POUM,
turns freedom fighters into fugitives,
slams foreign crusaders into germ-ridden prisons
to die from their wounds and ideals –
in the meantime Franco's Spanish rats
spill in through the chaos and wobbling lines
of faction-split fronts: Madrid, Aragón,
Málaga, Bilbao, Huesca, Barcelona,
Valencia; all fall like dominoes – blood
pours into Spain like wine from a porrón...

12.
Rats large as cats nibbling scraps
in Republican pannikins: new rule of kings
sets in with the twitch of liquorish moustache,
stamp of black boots, a yellow/red flag,
rumpus of tub-thumping Fascist salutes,
ustedes, Dons, Senores restored
with classes and castes, tips, brothels, profits,
private monopolies – only the oranges
glow the same colour, like paraffin lights
in ink-spilt night's genuflected trees.

Oranges are oranges under Republicans,
Socialists, Anarchists, Fascists, all –isms;
they all taste the same to rats, cats and kings.

First drafted 5th November 2004

———————————————

Notes:

Stanza 2:   ILP = Independent Labour Party
             'a tubercular scribbler...' = refers to George Orwell
             porrón = Spanish drinking vessel for wine

Stanza 3:   Ramblas = a mile-long promenade in Barcelona

	Usted = formal version of 'you' in Spanish – the Republicans occupying Barcelona altered such formal addressing of citizens to the informal, to emphasize equality; the Fascists preferred formal addresses
Stanza 7:	POUM = (Partido Obrero de Unificación Marxista) The Workers Party of Marxist Unification
	Fascistas maricones = Fascist poofs
Stanza 11:	¡Hola otra vez Barcelona! = 'Hello again Barcelona!' Maurín = leader of the POUM Confederación Nacional de Trabajo = (CNT) National Confederation of Workers *La Batalla* = pro-Fascist paper in Madrid Friends of Durruti = anarchist militia opposed to militarization and governmentalism in the peoples' militia Nín = co-founder of POUM who was falsely accused by the Communists of conspiring with the Fascists, and subsequently disappeared pannikins = metal containers for warming up food rations in and eating them from

A Mighty Absence

When she was fussing around him, throwing
Chocolate foil missiles while he tried to read,
Nudging his knee so his cradled book slipped
To his irritable sigh of 'Oh, Helen',
His word-anchored gaze longed for solitude.

But when she was working an afternoon shift
His books became milestones of hours,
Grave-heavy weights that heaped on his mind
And his cattle-grid brow; he'd stare into space
And the empty lounge which after a while
Took on all the gloom of his thoughts in her absence;
He'd shuffle about like an abandoned schoolboy,
Biting his nails while the minutes
Traipsed by like a regiment of plodding doubts;
His fresh-polished shoes standing neatly to attention
For inspection by an empty fireplace;
His whole soul missing her, hanging grey
And desolate in his face.

The Well and the Wisher

There father sat, fishing for wishes
In the plastic tub filled with soapy water,
Face weighed down by cattle-grid brow,
Sad and thundery, a bedraggled angler
With nothing to show for patience and strain,
No bend on the rod, at best a mere morsel
At the end of his line.

Scrubbing the Queens' heads till they gleamed
As if freshly minted; ELIZABETH REG revived
Into sudded sparkle – regal tender
To bag and exchange for pentagon-shaped
Tolls to slot in the electric metre.

He gazed at the coins at the bottom
Of the shallow plastic well, frothing
With washing-up liquid bubbles, but silent,
No more fulfilling wishes, only see-through bubbles
Swelling and bursting on the limpid surface.

Then looked again through his wobbled reflection
At layers of coins and saw for moments
Glistening copper-coloured pebbles
He'd try to fetch out from the bed of the stream
Trickling down through the sloping meadow
At the foot of his father's hill, as a boy;
In that clouded time he'd stare back to
The smallholding summit on the crinkly brow
And think: 'I wonder where I'll be
Fifty years from now'.

His dank reflection reformed in the pool
At his feet, now ditchwater green
For scum and mould shed from the coins
Like driftwood from a ship wreck.

His fingers fished the pebbles out
From the unreflecting stream.

The Luxury of Despair

How can my satisfaction last
In what can't last?
How can I look forward to the future
When all there is, is past?
What's the point in thinking infinite
When our actual lives are crimped within a limit?
What's the point in immortalising words
When poets only sing three scores, like birds?
Thoughts like these must be packed away
And slung over the shoulder for the working day;
Vast baggage stuffed into a bag
A fraction of their size,
But you have no choice – the lifelong snare –
You have to work to earn and to survive
So you can have the luxury of despair.

Dark, Sun and Thunder

Ask Miss Gayler's obscure nationality
A tardy answer would sniff and fuss
From her tight-lipped mouth: 'I'm Swiss', as if
No consequence, a rumpled quandary
Like the lumpy carpet hunchbacked by
The gap-foot of the front door;
Draught excluder by default
Stiffening the loose-hinged door,
Clamming visitors in its wedging clamp.

Miss Gayler kept her Jewishness
Between herself and Yahweh –
Nobody else's business besides –
In light of one anti-Semitic tenant,
House-troglodyte, who'd a stand-up line:
'How many Jews does it take to fit a light-bulb?
None: they contract it out to Gentiles!'

My enquiry: innocent curiosity,
Following up the near-tangible lead
Of her pronunciation; instinctual as
Prescribing chicken soup for a cold
Or tea as a tonic for nerves.
Nothing insidious in asking this question
As suggested her harassed black eyes.

'You open the window, I shut off the heating!'
Threatened an angry, lipless smile
Creasing darkly on tight, blanched skin
Like a damp patch on the yellowed hallway ceiling –
As Jehovah chucked locusts on Egyptians
Miss Gayler would punish us with cold;
Dish out Thou Shalt Nots with the rent books,
Each commandment engraved one to ten
On the cryptic papyri of her face.

This tumbled house, her Old Testament:
Faded, contradictory, stark;
Its wrath smote in chipped brick, flaking plaster,
Creaking banisters – had its own ghost,
A Cavalier cadaver politely haunting the landing
Centuries in rent arrears, lingering on
Like the stubbly, panda-eyed recluse
Walled-up in his fictions in a tiny, stuffed room
Replete in dusty armchair, wanderlust wardrobe
Shuffling about at night on its own.

Miss Gayler, Morgan La Fay of this day,
Animist witch, timetabled the sun
By rota so's not to saturate the bulbs
Or fade the lace curtains irreversibly beige;
Apollo at her beck and call, along with light-bulbs
Tingling forbiddingly in the musty front hall –
One burst and she saw it as God's mysterious
Way of saying: 'Don't flick the switch too quick!'

Prestigiously attentive to dust was Miss Gayler;
One pictured her dusting stuffed manikins
In monolith armchairs, inspecting fugitive
Fingertip-specks, gleaming with what
'Cleanliness is next to...' – ghosts seemed drawn
To her high standards: 'There's a woman in
A petticoat who sits in my bay-window smiling;
She doesn't scare me – she's quite beguiling. '

Her cobwebbed hair was once jet-black
As her liquorish eyebrows; horn-rimmed glasses
Magnified the hunted darkness of her eyes
When her ready temper rumble-tumbled on short cue
If wrong-footed by harmless enquiries:
'Which country are you from originally Miss Gayler?'
You learnt not to ask such questions of her

Once rebuked with a curt 'I'm Swiss'
Huffing out on her stale perfumed breath,
Face thunder-strained like the housekeeper
In her favourite film, *Rebecca*.

You felt guilt stoned in your throat,
Not yours to choke on; from a fruit
Rotting with Lilith in the front patio garden
Where rubble starved flowerpots of the light-giving brute:
An occasional sun, occasionally pouring on
Sad environs, empowered by its burden
Of solar Diaspora – quantum arsenal;
A macrocosmic blackmail stamped through the ages
Now dark sun and thunder in the heart of Miss Gayler.

Daddy-Long-Thoughts

Day of returns and returning, re-
visiting overgrown rails of the mind
played as a tangible, metaphoric trip
to Bognor Regis, on rickety tracks
to difficult pasts, disguised in green-washed
terraces, sleepy, ghostly arcades,
a cramped museum of only two rooms
stuffed with Nineteen Forties' nostalgia,
animistic wireless sets, old record players
safely remote in chameleon cases,
cabinets filled with hiss and song,
mahogany mausoleums of ghost voices
caught for posterity on vinyl like
life-lines on faces; promising returns
to muffled yesteryears, *take good care
of yourself, you belong to me* – and other legends:
Anything is possible with a cup of tea,
eternally-spiralling memory
caught in stylus-rut-tut of thought –
Dad taps into service days' airwaves
transported back to Signaller duties
tapping his name on the Morse-code machine,
last ditched attempt, unconsciously,
to communicate with his obsessive mouse-wife
cowering in a dark hole in the wainscoting.

Billeted at Barnham with baggage of years'
tortuous travelling to begin again
life's recurring evacuation
to flutters of breeze-leafed luggage tags,
tell-tale stickies of the soul –
the mighty distance lived, giant stones
of vast, towering things experienced,
time-manipulating milestones of minutes
morphing to trees, fields, hedges, clouds

in capitulation with the past,
pantomiming, re-performing moments
lost mostly in hope of non-remembering,
forgetfulness, vital blinkers
of present-seeking senses of cross-each-bridge-
as-you-come-to-it now; off-putter of tomorrow.

In the musty existing room of my parents,
crammed full with family mementos, books,
photographs, Styx's toll-fare tokens
or the hold of a Pharaoh's morbid tomb,
crouch Eden's forgotten descendants, once giants
now shrivelled into earthly, miniature size
like two toy-scale figures in a rented dolls' house
sandwiched between a struggling back garden
and windowed partition to the outside world –
ghosts haunting progress's tumbleweeding suburbs,
eyes seamed with crow's-feet, stitched under-shadows
stewed-tea grey; old-shoe-brown pupils
glistening tiredness, penetrating as nerves
jarred between contrapuntal cogs
of thought, strung out by crippling
preoccupations of the moment,
terror's cryptic puzzles, silent shouts
skirting-board-shrunk inversely in size
to towering effect; nerves' stretched piano wires
creaking lost chords, lost notes, lost times;
eyes strained as recycled tea-bags, marbled
as milk-swirling tea, or egg-whites
bubbling in a frying-pan shrapnelled with shell-
splinters; ancestral tut-tut of out
-of-kilter clock stuck forever at Six –
tea-time to starch-scented Edwardians –
illustrates to etiquetteless ear
what on some other plane struggles to be heard
in deafening, daytime, stuffy lounge silence,
dins of the taxidermist's inner-ear:
cork-creaking minutes, stone-scraping seconds –

Time is fed up, it's fretting, it's biting
its nails, until the next train comes.

Tea brings lapsed contentment, tings spirits
presently depleted to muster stimulation,
stir peculiarly back into being
like pink-striped Bagpuss in his sepia shop,
caffeine-revivified, resuscitated to
stammers of nerve-edged conversations,
verbal grabbling for mental distraction,
reiterated interests stale with taste-betraying
syllables, dull, insipid, yellowed eye
watery weak; drained; stewed; drunk on spurts
of recaptured happier times flitting
fuzzy as bulb-clunking moths;
suicidal daddy-long-thoughts birthed by lullabies
of a moment's beyond self-soothing rocks
of tense torsos, time-tripping sighs,
excruciating tocks.

Depending on mood my Dad's a Mad Hatter
postulating posterity's teatime scraps –
as the dirty armchairs draped in sun-blanched covers
darken to monoliths, immovable doubts
in unexpected thunder-gloom cast by a cloud,
he turns to Mock Turtle, too life-tired to cry;
my mother alternates between March Hare
and Dormouse, depending on the hold
of sudden grope of hope or insoluble obsession
in the dimly gas-lit dolls' house of her mind –
we take our places in listless mummery
of past thoughts, feelings, imprisoning meanings
breathing back to life through thawing of sighs,
interminably frequent tripping of time...
More dishwater tea? asks Dormouse Mother
of Mad Hatter father to teapot patter;
she yaffles affirmations, *yawf – yawf – yawf,*

nearest her mouth comes to forming *yes*
since aeons of negatives; rings tea-strained eyes;
lapses back to doubt-muttered sleepy-byes,
rinsed of all energies; timeless tea-party
tripping with lethargy, rusting gentility,
frozen forever at Six-'O'-Clock,
stirring the stewed tea with my watch.

Angst-ridden glances grappling ungraspables –
tripped up by a thought's footstool –
go in circles round the centre table plinth –
casting story spells like the pacing Bronte sisters –
a jaundiced tomato plant implores its luminous
green buds to blush red, red of our tied blood
binding us together in eternal trinity,
chains of pulsing rosary beads
itching to hatch from vinegared shells
like November conkers; domestic mysteries
probed, unsolved, self-defining; ruby
red of veins causing on wilderness-verged
tracks like spidering varicose trains.

Miss Discombobulated

Wearing laundry of years, two holes
for eyes where blackbirds pecked the linen
lined with experience's permanent creases,
she clung to the word 'discombobulated'
as if a thick, warm, comfortable fur-coat;
trampled years since contented
with hyperbole of 'moments' reeking like
cheap white wine in a lukewarm glass;
her past, a fug of pub fag-smoke
perfuming her black Hispanic hair;
ages since pages she once wrote
saw shimmer of day; memories'
invisible walls stalled her everywhere.

Shell Shock

A huddled, bedraggled sand-bag,
eyes trembling with special fear
born from fatigue and lack of fags;
body crouched west but canny of rear

guns rattling from the unseen east,
gattling chatter of bucolic bronchitis –
lungs concertina with grampus wheeze
of book-dust asthma, pen-hand arthritis –

in No-Fags-Land the casualties
of dregs-shovelled roll-ups scatter the carpet
of umber mud; battlefield teas
spill on the listing parapet

of warping pamphlets' ducking curves
under bombardments of battered nerves.

A Letter from David Kessel

His crabbed handwriting scrawls
'poetry is a savage war'
and other pills of pub beer wisdom:
'in the destructive element immerse!'
straight from the disinherited Lord Jim
with a suicidal, sherbet-tasting bite
like the powder spilt out on the numbing tongue
from the split capsule of an anti-depressant;
jagged scrawls crawl on the page
collaged by spider legs of tobacco.

'I'm still out of touch' the swatted legs
of insects spell out on the off-white paper,
'and, I believe, over-medicated!'
but not too much to date the letter –
'I'll leave it there' the scribbles say
'be in touch soon   Yours truly'
then his squashed spider appears:
'David' makes arachnophobics flinch
and all the flies trapped in the spinning years.

O The Windows of the Bookshop Must Be Broken*
For David Kessel

Is that the Cockney poet who sings splintered cities
Sat, a damp jackdaw, on a bench-perch there,
Succouring a spindly, smoking twig? Licked
Rhetoric: I recognised him at first sight;
Or myself through the gulled glass of a parallel life –
So this was what obscure compassion looked like:

Moony, two-way mirror eyes, fogged with thought,
Reflecting ghosted furniture of the room,
Wall shadows; the soul of the muttering door;
Obscurities crimped in schizophrenic things:
Animist glimpses of the chronically nerved –
Channelled through sentiment object-projected;
Tangible triggers re-shaping blanched traumas.

Face: sallow, sunless, shade of curdled tea,
Faintly lit with sincerity's buttercup glow;
Flashes of a harassed child – Little Time grown up
In hand-down, tight, untranslatable insights –
A sheep-eyed Leopold Bloom in itching hair-shirt;
The conscientious misanthrope every city needs;
The ghostly conscience stalking visceral streets;
Dreaming giro stories to capsize pickled lives;
Tapping Socialism trapped in bricked-up histories
Of peeling terraces – lust corrosive as spit
Rusting the tongue that would taste the world
But for hampering of pill-slugged speech.

'Do you see yourself as a survivor?' I ask in another voice –
'Me? I suppose I am...surviving', he stammers
Adding, as an afterthought, often left just that:
'I'm chronic!' More emphatic than a big, black, monstrous,
Insurmountable full stop: *I am chronic.*

O but Captains cluster in his dampened spirit:
Saints with cluttered brows: Noonan, Keir Hardie
Ghosting sunless skin; shivered inspiration;
Obscurity can't trample down the Muse-struck tramp,
He tramples on to saddle-stitched skies...
It's true thoughts' Pillar'd Mansions shrink on paper –
The gamble's to be published and still stand,
Better the salvation of the page –
The printed line forfeit for interpretation –
Time to reclaim The Means of Publication –
O the windows of the bookshop must be broken!

* from Glass Is Dynamite, by David Kessel

Keir Hardie Street
Allan Jackdaw (1891 – 1917)

i. Dick Whittington's City

Gash of grubby red-brick buildings
Under bruise of urban sky –
In every doily-curtained windows lives a life –
Motionless stout spectators crouch, watch the trains heave in,
Black bricks of Battersea do the steam proud,
Steeplejack chimneys tousle to attention,
Colobus clouds swing from chimney to chimney:
A tumbling audience stirring fresh from concrete beds,
First fags of the day
Chimney from drainpipe-brimmed trilbies.

Tock-o-clock in the morning, too early to tell the time;
Through lifting fogs peeling back like greying scabs
City pricks up higgledy-piggledy against Calvary skyline:
A pencil smudge of gaswork cloud bruising on the paper arm
Of the street urchin pale, pearly horizon,
Soon brushed away by the charlady sun.

Black-mouthed London, charred chimney sweep
Spluttering soot; dark tubercular blood;
Guttersnipe city – barely the room
For a thought to cough to a word,
Funnelled as smoggy zephyrs through
Gap-toothed stucco terraces,
Plaque-caked like the yellow screeching teeth
Of a Jack-stalked slattern, flapping down
Daisy,   Daisy   airless backstreets
With asthmatic, *Lambeth Walk*, music hall effort;
A lost, panting tramp in labyrinth pitch
Gin-soaked to the skin, barrelling out
Roll out the Barrels as he Rag-And-Bones by.

ii. Short Shanks the Shopkeeper

On Betterton Street, Old Short Shanks Joe
Stirs to the salts of his wife's soapy hands
Offering a Rosy Lee libation
Steaming sweet, piping brown
Like the Ganges in Kiplin's In'ja –
Rushed sips, kippers, crockery clanks;
Slap of lather for junket-thick shave,
Scrape, scrub, scrape, scrub, scrub-a-dub-dub –
Punctual as tulips is this old Buff –
Time to puff up, peel on his slippers,
Flip-flop and trip down the Apples and Pears
Lift up the shutters of the shut-eye shop –
Hosiery, drapery, haberdasher, collibosher –
Time to butter up more bread and honey
With a *Knees up Mother Brown* and a bish, bash, bosh!

Polishes his clobber
Spanking clean and dapper for Daisy   day,
All manner of hats, all shapes and spats,
Whistles *My Old Man's a Dustman* as
His hoarded goods dust up spick and spam;
Old Joe only takes notes, crisp from franking,
No credit or slates in his kind of banking –
Worked his way up from poor shop apprentice
To flush haberdasher with a ledger for saving –
Scrimped and scraped for this crust of a chance
To pass to his sons his scrimpings and scrapings.

Long ago when Short Shanks was just a wistful titch
In shorter hoes, mince pies glitter-bright
And life-is-but-a-dream-blue,
He filled this dismal city with laughter running through
Pigeon-parting streets
Taking the wind and laundry with him,

The sombre peals of sad St. Paul's,
The striking chimes of glum Big Ben –
Blew them up in a paper bag and burst them!

So full of big, brassy band-stand grand ideas,
Fishing possibilities in the ditchwater-green,
Pummelled lustre of his shimmering Thames,
Glinting like a twitching chevalier's armour:
The city's next Dick Whittington,
Rags-to-riches rise to power
And with that power, O what mighty deeds:
He'll level this higgledy-piggledy city,
So tramps have more attentive tailors;
Workhouses, slums fill with life and laughter;
Churches used by old rich folk
To pay daily penitence in head-down prayers
Till their dromedaries shrink needle-size;
Shopkeepers, landlords offer alms
To the downtrodden left; ill-gotten profits
Put back in bellies of hungry customers,
No more cap-in-hand – now slate-in-gait...

Something then occurred to him
While shinning up his self-assembled ladder:
'What if', instead of cutting down this beanstalk,
I stops right here and opens up a shop?
With a fee fie foe and fiddle-dee-fum
He polishes his nest-egg, sells it on,
Builds himself a brick-and-mortar castle,
All terrace and turret, sets to work
To Capitalise on fortune, shore up profits,
Still promising himself, unlike Mister Kipps,
He'll not forget his promise, why he begun this:
To make enough to share with the starved,
The dispossessed, the workhouse mice –
But before he sets to this transformation
Of his slum-sunken, broken-spirit city,
Needs-must bake enough dough to leaven it with bread.

But when the day comes he's got enough to spare,
Married with three nippers, a fourth'n on the way,
Such a busy man, managed to expand
So's he pays two boys a pittance wage
To run his rag-shop for him while
He gains weight and cigars,
Comfy cushion days plotting mighty schemes
To expand his little empire, swell its bounteous borders,
Incorporate more shops, more boys, more trade,
But most of all make sure nothing's given
Without the promise of more in return –
'Trouble with old Robin Hood,' thinks Joe,
'He had no business sense – I must
Shore up me' capital, lift me' offspring up
To a better level than slums I sprouted from!'

The city, his kith, but who'd favour cousins
Over closer kin? His empire would pass
To his eldest son per primogeniture
To build on it in turn for his own children,
A dynasty spawned, one with common touch,
Nostalgia for downtrodden origins:
Its alms embrace Charity, inflate Church funds
With copyrighted coffers, orphans parish-sponsored
To shadow Steeple Sweepers; workhouse Chars
Gifted brand new mops; damned tramps handed
Dry pairs of togs; wreaths made of lilies-
of-the-gutter, laid on dromedaries of rag-bone carts
Trailed by processions of grateful underdogs
Lusting piping soup kitchens
To be baptised in gin, brimstone and broth –
'All this generosity to be ladled out by me:
I'll patent it Shanks's Charity!'

What's become of Short Shanks since?
He's prospered, passed on through the needle's eye
'cross Thames' Styx to Heaven's Pillar'd Halls –

His kith and kin keep building high,
Lost touch with the common ground,
Legions of ants in a brush's bristles,
Lost sight of microscopic battles
Of citizens who've lost sight of the sky
For marble towers blotting it from view;
Draping from scaffoldings like public laundry
Banner-legends fly: You Too
Can Scale These Heights If You Grit Your Nose
To the Grindstone – Profit as You'd Be Profited By!
Stash Your Four and Twenty Blackbirds in the Right Pie!

iii. Three True Obscuritans

– *The Hermit of Hercules Buildings*

Once heard tales of an unfashionable recluse
Hid like a fiend in Hercules Buildings,
Thirty years or more;
His curtains never twitched to spy
Inspiration in people-bustled streets:
His was in-growing; head-clouds parted daily
Gifting insights into all things: Visions
Of lost Albion, Jerusalem grass-green
Growing in the grimy, gin-fumed streets
And airless *Daisy,*   *Daisy* alleyways;
Emerald wisteria climbing dirt-brick walls,
Seeking sunlight like a thinker seeks the truth –
A resurrecting Eden strangling black chimneys
With seething creepers, gloriously blemishing
Wren's Capital of marble in forests of mouldering trees –

They say Mister Blake rarely left his digs
Except at night when nightingales warbled
On the chattering Heath, then to consult
With Angels and shoulder-perched fleas

As to details of limitless prophecies,
Nothing but tobacco and Eastern teas
To stimulate the Hampstead Shaman –
Thirty-odd years with the curtains drawn
So light from within could burst un-assuaged;
No noise but the squeak and creak of his press
Printing each word in indelible ink
Impressed on our minds ever since –
Why should one who strides with Angels care
Whether his works see daylight; spine-
Crack like brittle leaves in autumn air?

– *The Turpentine Prophet*

I've a dream-fired friend, struggling writer,
Pure spit and spirit, distemper, turpentine,
Can't sell his novel 'cause publishers won't read it
Unless the manuscript is put in type –
He's got Socialism thumping in his heart,
Rumbling like a thunder in his belly,
But for all his revolutionary fervour,
Still must bow his knees to earn his crust –
As he does for the unleavened on his Sundays –
Eighteen hour days painting walls of betters,
Plastering and filling up the cracks,
While like-ravines ravage his scamped hands
Chiselling his physsog with fatigue –
A messianic journeyman with cultured sensibilities
Reduced to scrimping from menial means
A second coat of matt Socialist vision –
A skidder on a class-transcending mission,
His workmates strip him down – they'll not listen:
Prefer to scamp their makeshift lives
Shoddily coating bricks of a prison,
Slaking on stout, plastered as Paris;
Place depleting capital on deceptive bets,
Slave to keep themselves in bread and cigarettes –

No thoughts on fighting for the right of labour
To employ their souls and minds as well as bodies;
No burning desire in their turpentine hearts
To rent sublime swirls, twirling intricacies
Of flora on wallpaper they sloppily paste
To peel and blister: the patterns of waste.

– The Ghost of a Poet

Another friend, should say the ghost of one,
Suffered much, swallowed pride's stale crust,
Him and his flint-and-roses missus,
Something borrowed bond, and something blue,
Doing without for scrimped months at a time
So's he could turn his poverty to poetry –
Little in the two words after all –
Before his calloused hands blueberried up from graft
To grip something gentlemanly as a pen;
A tool, let's not forget, more suited to
Pianist-like spatulas of better furnished men.
Was it worth it? Yes, each bitter, bleeding line;
But meagre recognition of tepid-inked reviews
Scarce enough to save him from his cancer fancies,
So he hurled himself from off a Cornish cliff,
A poet in his prime of death;
Leaving his flinty trouble-and-strife sixty bob in savings,
Double what they'd giftedly eke
On an average, tummy-grumbling week.

– Those Intractable Art Martyrs

Only hope of recognition for their paper labours
Posthumous, I'll bet you, it'll come
Decades down the Circle line of time,
Long past their unmarked paupers' graves
Nameless as that unknown Tommy's tomb
Who got it in the cork from a Dervish poking fork –

Leave ghosted legacies in inner-city cemeteries,
No towering memorials to soldiers of the pen and brush;
Only those receptive to clamouring cries
Of spiritual picket-lines – Bow Bells of the other side –
To witness their mute protests, blank placards,
Haunting the Abbey with spectral petitions
To be with the Remembered in that Corner –
A Purgatory of posthumous spectating
How, short of shouting red sedition
Like Marx from the pulpit of Speakers' Corner,
Could self-respecting hair-shirts scrimp crusts of consolation
From dead-ends of idealistic minds?
Nagging conviction: *It IS possible!*
John Lilburne proselytised so;
Winstanley set digging its foundations
And might have wrestled up the roots but for blight
Of spiked Putney debates dousing his light
Shining, a time, in Buckinghamshire;
The Chartists and Unions clamoured for its cause;
Keir Hardie fused its inspiration to exact
Literate leaps and bounds of a dauntless autodidact –
Might have made it had our burgeoning numbers
Taken up suffrage, not invitations
To pontificating parties' teapot politics
Where Mr. Quintus Fabius did the pouring;
The intricate clatters of crockery on trays:
Idle silver singers of cake-stand days.

iv. The Sea-Green Line

I commuted along the City and South London;
Not retreat, digress, a mental pilgrimage
In electric-flickered carriage underground
To find new perspectives on the glum city above,
Alight at the ghost station of my conscience
In shadows of Progress' echoing tomb...
Followed the stations on the curved roof carriage:

MOORGATE...OLD STREET...ANGEL....KING'S CROSS...

Hours clattered by, found myself dazed
On sepulchral platform whose designated name
Had yet been assigned – lost, stumbled blind
Through combing catacombs, labyrinthine tunnels
Circling tile-scaled walls, till I tripped
Onto another nameless platform, un-haunted –
Then out the char-black mouth of the howling tunnel,
The elephantine roar of an approaching monster
Screeching into view on the track trailing tongue
From the tunnel's mouth – the metallic Leviathan
Heaved slowly to a halt, hissing, sniffing
Like a mighty, miffed Trojan bull;
I entered with trepidation sealing myself in –
Soon as seated the carriage gathered pace,
Whisking me into darkness undiscovered.

On the carriage wall the artery of this line
Bled from black to a sea-green shade,
So it appeared in the light's moth-hovered glow –
To my dumbfounded sights I read the names
Of ghost stations not heard of before,
Not in all my days in this dreary city –
Were they building another City, underground?
The next stop tantalisingly called
LILBURNE COMMON – then, WINSTANLEY ROAD,
I scanned along: ROBERT OWEN JUNCTION,
SMILLIE CIRCUS, PANKHURST SQUARE –
I'd discovered another London off the Sea-Green Line
Where black City and Metropolitan purple fused
Like two honing arteries at the cardio-junction
Of the beating heart of another city
Only accessed through the tube – alighted
To discover what alternative city waited over-ground
At the summit-light of the spiralling stairway.

v. The Secret City

First thing that struck my startled pies
Blinking in to sunlit vision,
The cleanness of the pavements and streets;
Tall stucco terraces towering high immaculate
Like mighty marble monuments,
Vast statues built to stand the test of time and tribulation,
Lived-in by levelled citizens, each
Of equal, immutable importance to their city;
A splinter of the city-Soul, vital shard
In the vibrant sparks of productive industry
Catering for all, furnishing lives
With mortal comforts plenty, to empower
The people on a level ground so they might strive for skies
Of spiritual nourishment, develop dormant faculties
Neglected long ago in dark Capital times
When Mister Bloggs pilfered his neighbour's crust,
Cajoled profits, fattened his coffers
Not for great works' public benefit
But for its own in-growing pleasure –

This new secret City built on compassion's
Incorruptible foundations, indomitably shod –
On each terrace innumerable names
Etched in the stone, beatific tributes
To lives breathing within the slabs of brick:
Here lives Mr and Mrs Such-n-such
Who mortar bricks with happiness and laughter;
Here lives the Such-n-suches who share each day
Making cakes rise with optimistic conversations;
Here live some children who photograph their dreams
To inspire their sleeping parents;
Here dwells a family mesmerised
By swirling dreams wallpapering their days;
So bright inscriptions spread throughout singing streets
And billboards bore new slogans:
"GIVING IS LIVING, LIVING IS GIVING; "

"THE CAMEL STALLS AT THE NEEDLE'S EYE";
"MONEY IS THE ROOT OF ALL ENMITY";
"PROPHETS, NOT PROFITS"; "TRUE WORK EMPLOYS
OUR SOULS AND MINDS'; "FILL YOUR HOUSE
WITH WHAT IS BEAUTIFUL AND USEFUL'...

I, startled tourist, now panting breathless
In delight at stumbling on this lost Utopia –
What pleased me most, the absence of shops
Or haggling markets, crash of trading tills,
No more cons of cash for faulty objects
Or food past best, no wheeler-dealing
In dodgy goods past kosher quota,
No stealing or need for any thieving,
No tricks or cons on browsing customers,
Trusting or desperate – this city has no desperate –
Public services publicly run,
Never before had I seen so many trams!

An absence of pubs for people punch-drunk
On conversation: *'course you know why they've never
Got round to a revolution in the other London, don't you?
It's tea, that's what it is. Makes 'em apathetic,
Complacent-like; summin in the brew –
It's their Spiritual Gin 'see, make no bones about it
– This is it...
Gin was never so in-si-di-ous as tea is,
Makes you feel all warm inside, content in your place
– This is it...
Without the educative need next day
For a hair of the dog – 'Course havin' said that
I miss it meself, 'speshly in the mornins,
– Oh yes...
But gettin' up to a salmon-sky dawn, no false one,
Nippers singing in the streets, whole bleedin' city
Greetin' you as one big happy fam'ly – none of this
Flesh 'n' blood lark they string out back there,
No, here your neighbour's as like your brother,*

N' we all muck in togever, for common good,
No nippers squealing with empty bellies, no poverty,
– This is it…
Nah. I can get by without tea.

This secret London: Society of intelligence
Prised long by pamphlet-thumbing Fabian firesides
And planted in coal miners' torch-haloed heads,
Now a sharp reality, well-defined as sun,
A hovering pit-lamp in the white night sky:
By the time on my watch it was well past nine
At night, yet daylight poured its yolk on stucco turrets
Glistening with magic promise, urban Camelot
Captured in blazing daubs as if by Pre-Raphaelite
Brush on white-glossed canvas; shimmering
Ideality; poetry tangibly manifest
In this unlikeliest of cities – a Parousia
Of pillar boxes, pigeons and fairground laughter.

vi Keir Hardie Street

Then – well stone the crows! I scarce believed
My pies as I beheld the street's bright sign:
KEIR HARDIE STREET in pristine white
Ivory lettering on glistening coal black;
For minutes the shining white letters dazzled me
Till I felt I'd topple from the kerb, tumble off
Like Whittington with his tags and baggage
Billeted with classless scraps and famished cat
Only to rise and prosper – a vision I had
Lit up before me in piercing mist on this street,
Of its gifted namesake, his pit-face rise
From Dark Satanic collieries, Caledonian obscurities,
Into light of politics, calloused hand campaigning,
Who strove to lift the people with winging words,

Help all prosper, not just his kith and kin
And own interests but emphatically the whole –
Humanity primo franca , descended
From the dust and ribs of Common-held Eden
Corrupted by tilted scales of serpentine greed
Hissing its syllables: *Capitalism*
Spouting from billboards on peeling city walls
Whilst Socialism mutters to itself in draughty halls!

In Whittington's city, 'mongst the Pillar'd Mansions
Of Wren's grand vistas and esplanades,
Another fire catching the wind ignited
Not in Pudding Lane, but Lanarkshire,
Its touch paper smoking in the undernourished clutch
Of a baker's cadaverous delivery boy
Waylaid amid errands by sudden lightning flash
Striking him down in well-trammelled tracks
As that streak did to Paul on his way to Damascus!

Down the line from Communist Christ,
'Head Leveller', as coined his cousin Baptist,
(Though one might trace right back to Solon's
Shaking Off of Burdens, Seisaktheia)
A line of Social Soldiers, Outlaws, Prophets
Strove to oppose Rule of Profits,
Chivalrously crying Redistribution!
Thomas Beckett itching with idealisms in
His hair-shirt, sandling beggars' feet;
Robin Goodfellow in Lincoln-green hood
Stilling the bow-hand; Thomas More
Dreaming castles in the air where citizens lived
According to their needs, not wants, a doctrine
Of dock-leaf and ditchwater practised by
Roger Crabb, the original Mad Hatter
Who gave his hat-profits to the poor;
The Black and Sea Greens' proselytising;
The Buckinghamshire Diggers striving

To plough cloddish thoughts of Arden anew;
Robert Owen's Chartists; Messianic miners;
Marx's Synoptic Social Gospels
Long-pantomimed in low pews and high-brow bowers
Where the Rich man shared his hymns
With trembling soap-hands of Fabians;
Where ever the Parson went hand in hand
With the Mammon alms of the Owner of Land:
From this union of penny-pinching piety
Sprung the Molloch we term as Charity!

Time again for Commoners' crop-head opposition
To titled Abusers of Privilege,
Not seen since old Roundhead times:
For a sullen and scowling class sitting apart
Is preferable to a besotted and unthinking class
Dragged hither and thither by unscrupulous guides. *

Turn the other cheek We may,
But after we've over-turned the rustling tables
And spilt the stinging metals to the floor,
Turned stone to bread, water into wine,
Sent camels packing back out through the needle's eye
Along with class, property, tyrannies of Kings
Until the grind and clamour of industry is mute
And we hear Angels singing to the sound of dropping pins.

vii. News from Somewhere

The vision's light faltered into darkness where it shrank,
Flickering dimly: now haloed a pit lamp
In whose wavering flicker a slave-black hand
Scratched Arabesque characters with a pin on coal wall,
Thereupon paraded what might be misconstrued
As primitive cave etchings, the concentrating hand
Breathing life into menageries of shorthand shadow-animals
(Was this the etymology for Pitman?) –

Once the pin-scratched scripture was shod
His gollywog lips blew the coal-dust away
Like a lady to avoid her letter blotting.

This vision soon returned its sparkled focus
Glinting, a silver plate catching the sun,
Whitening my sight: I saw a gloomy street
In place of that bright, brilliant one before,
To a slightly built, dowdy young man
Hunched before a bookshop window
Squinting his dot eyes at picture books
Tantalisingly spine-spread before him:
James Keir Hardie strained to read printed fictions
At the tail-end of autodidactic mission –
But he'd also learnt to read between the letters
Of untold stories, editors' omissions!

Fired by spark of sensed injustice first hand
This street's namesake threw off Calvinism's shirt,
Its two tier saved/damned parallels to class
And learnt to speak in temperance meetings,
Then politics: Member for North-West Ham,
Took his seat in Parliament in blue Scotch cap and tweeds;
Mrs. Grundy almost fainted when
She scanned the costume of the new-comer*
But for her smelling salts –
So offended by this chiselled, bearded pauper
Replete in blue serge double-breasted jacket,
Fawn-coloured trousers, striped flannel shirt,
Scarf tied round collar in a sailor's knot.

There stood shabbily-clad young Keir
Gifted this insight into his own future,
Oh what a story it promised to be;
His brown-dot pies squinted further to read
His yet-to-happen histories riveting his eyes
On the breathless pages in the bookshop window:
Sent down the coal mine when a bit laddie of eight…

Unable to sign his name on the membership pledge
Of the Good Templers… so ashamed he set to work
To learn to write… – what lightning he'd write –
The fisherfolk apostles in the New Testament
Would find themselves more at home in the company
Of Keir Hardie than in any other member of the House…
Emphatically a man of the future… of course,
For here he was reading his own mapped future
As all seers deem their mysterious right to do,
And what sententious, storm-filled speeches,
Thundering Das Kapital-bashing sermons
He'd holler from his pulpit bench in Parliament
To the battering of his calloused fists:
The still small voice of Jesus the Communist
Stole over the earth like a soft refreshing breeze
Carrying healing wherever it went…*

Then in a stroke he tumbled down by the mighty blow
Of pugilist opponents' vocal wrecking-ball;
A drubbing by the jingoes! A frightened gasp
Came from the mouth of the ragamuffin stooped
By the bookshop window, loaves in arm,
Smudge of breath on the sunless glass
That started melting before him, trickling
Back to grains of sand till dissolved away
Stripping the books of their glass palisade;
Long-un-fingered, tantalising pages
Wrestling in the warm wind of the streets
Struggling with muscles of pugilist gusts
Turning swiftly page by page
As Keir's hungry eyes read fast
Without pause for their enraptured need
Of published future, not posthumous,
Precognitive – but the ending petered out:
In his twilight years, having been first
Labour Leader, thence having passed on
The baton to another; a harassed old white-haired
Lion of politics, Aslan of Socialism

Fatally mauled
By the mocking goblins in the Commons,
Crawling into retirement's den
'Mid mundane thuds of book-packing –
Books marked birth, death and the bit in-between
For centuries; life is, was, had always been
One bookend-ed shelf – but now the books were free
Flying into the streets with a flapping of pages
For words were always meant as wings
To lift humanity, or prolong Its hesitation –
What hope without imagination?

Dreams and ideas are still staple diet
Of the more thoughtful of those lacking clothes and food,
Social prospects and education –
Plus opiums past, present and future:
Religion's 'moth-eaten brocade' for one,
Not forgetting that manipulated, sour-mouthed monster
Politics, Behemoth of the Modern,
Rung-grasping Grappler of the social climber
From Parliamentarians down to Whigs,
Fluttered the banners of Social Justice
With scamping small print whispering:
'Oneupmanship for All; All for Oneupmanship' –

Only manifestoes scratched out through
Hard grafted truths of injustice at first hand
Ever meant what they said and what they said
Was all they meant, no scrimp-print clause;
Now one such scribe, before his time,
Witnessed the truth too stark lightning-bright
To be inked on paper – the books were spilling
Out on the street, pages winging
Into flocks of paper doves tumbling
Throughout the pin-silent Pillar'd Mansions,
Tree-lined vistas, levelled esplanades
Of this inimitable City; little Keir,

Scruffy, unkempt as a guttersnipe from Dickens,
Knelt on the ground to finger pages
Of soft-bound books apparently blank,
Blissfully free of the weight of inked words –
Something like a fresh summer breeze
Ruffled out from the fluttering pages;
Its only words, a title: *News from Somewhere,*
First and last bound product of a Classless State
Where the Public controlled the Means of Publication.
Up got little Keir, white face no more
Knitted with quandaries born from injustice,
His eyes seemed shining, edified, free
Of resentments of darker times; now he,
And I – stood mind-lit on a corner –
Could see clearly with illumined pies
The point was to do not preach or write
Beliefs, but enact like dream-soldiers of old
In deed as well as speech; words can't be
Ends in themselves; to aim for the dream
Is the path to perfection, the dream put in us
To inspire us in building Lilburne and Blake's
Jerusalem from the rubble of Satanic Mills,
Just as our cloud-cousins did with this spirited
City turned upside down, shored up
The track of time down the Sea-Green Line,
Where folk glide off the ground on wings
For there's no need for feet
On KEIR HARDIE STREET.

Notes:

* quotes from Mr. Kier Hardie M.P., W. T. Stead (ed.), Coming Men on Coming Questions No: VI, (May, 18, 1905).
'moth-eaten brocade': from 'religion: that vast moth-eaten brocade', Aubade by Philip Larkin.

Allan Jackdaw is a fictious alter-ego of the author, a motif personifying the struggling working-class writer, based loosely on poet John Davidson ('Thirty Bob A Week') and novelist Robert Tressell *(The Ragged Trousered Philanthropists)*.

INDEX

A Day at the Council Estates	31	Gasping	75
A Hamper from Landrake	37	Giving Light	Back Poem
A Letter from David Kessel	147	Grandma's Ingredients	91
A Mighty Absence	134	Heirlooms	99
A Photo of Vaughan Williams	80	Hell or a Better Hand	90
A Summer Night's Travels	25	Hell's Full of Early Risers	120
Adam's Nib	72	Identifying Tim	86
Aneurin	101	In Search of the Haggard Ghost	15
At Least Tomorrow's Wednesday	124	In The Laps of the Gods	78
Beatitudes	84	In The Mist	85
Biography of a Ghost	90	Infatuation: The First	38
Brain Smoker	73	Infinite Things	91
Candles and Anglicans	43	Innocence Twisted	82
Captain Parker's Trunk	56	Intrusive Thoughts	83
Catching Sight of the Urban Fox	49	Jerome's Last Judgment	116
Chasing Shadows	82	Keir Hardie Street	150
Composing by Post	77	Last of the Spray Carnations	61
Cradle to Grave	88	Life's Brief	53
Daddy-Long-Thoughts	141	Little Hells	46
Dance of the Dragonflies	16	Lover's Tiff	52
Dark Advice	70	Make Way	19
Dark, Sun and Thunder	138	Martin Goth	118
Dead Reminder	98	Meeting the Paint Eater	73
Death in the Height of Summer	48	MIGHT	99
Death of a Socialist	100	Miss Clarke's Finishing School	79
Death Wears a Homburg	86	Miss Discombobulated	145
Death's Breathtaking View	54	Missing Ism	99
Destiny	30	Mist	88
Dole and Genealogy	22	Moleskin Man	76
Don't Envy the Empty Sun	81	Mother Mouse	45
Faith Flowers	89	My Life in the Shade	32
Few Never Envy	28	Nostalgia	13
Five Minute Infinity	85	O The Windows of the Booshop Must Be Broken*	148
Flowers in the Vase	87	Oblivions	91
Footnotes on Faith	89	Obverbs	67
Forgive-Me-Not	Front poem		

Old-Fashioned Sun	35	The Luxury of Despair	137
Only Rosie Smokes	113	The Mansion Gardens	17
Orange & White	84	The Need to Dream Forever	96
Per Mare Per Terrum	78	The Old Pianos	78
Poem on Empty	96	The Poet Tree	81
Rats, Cats and Kings	126	The Renewers	114
Reversing Charges	105	The Ring	36
Riddle of the Sphinx	100	The Rosary Beads	41
RIP Lives	75	The Sound of Eating	102
Shell Shock	146	The Stain	98
Signature like a Squashed Spider	72	The Sunday Poem	72
Spilt Milk	82	The Water Shallows	13
Spiritual Gin	47	The Well and the Wisher	135
Sui Oblitus Commodi	110	Three Scores and Tea	117
Tales from the Empty Larder	33	Timétations	92
The Backpacker	74	i. The Bin of Time	
The Battle of Trafalgar Street	76	ii. Time Bites	
The Blackboard	82	iii. Closing Time	
The Brain of God	87	iv. White	
The Buzzard	71	v. Out of Clock Time	
The China Kingfisher	27	vi. Old Father Time	
The Coin Foragers	97	vii. Time Anxiety	
The Commuter Belt	106	vii. The Clock That Forgot the Time	
The Commuter's Last Stop	51	ix. Little Father Time	
The Corn Thresher	20	Victuals	103
The Cottage	34	i. Transubstantiation	
The Dark and Keir Hardie	101	ii. Holy Roofs	
The Drive	83	iii. Communion	
The Fade	105	iv. The Absence of Butterflies	
The False Confession	40	White Collar Rhyme	77
The Glove Compartment	44		
The Gospels of Gordon Road	62		
The Guilty Building	80		
The Haunted Ghosts	97		
The House of Sadness Past	58		
The House on the Rise of Reversion	14		
The Linger of Yearning	105		

Acknowledgements

Aesthetica, Airings, Awen, Bard, Candelabrum, Carillon, Decanto, Echoes of Gilgamesh, Eclipse, The Engine, Eratica, Exile, First Time, Great Works, Headstorms, Illuminations (international), Jacobyte Poetry, Monkey Kettle, The Once Orange Badge Poetry Supplement, Pennine Platform, The Penniless Press, The People's Poet, Poetic Hours, Poetry Express, Poetry Now, Poet Tree, Pulsar, Seeker, Snakeskin, South, Strix Varia, Taj Mahal Review, Voice & Verse, The Yellow Crane.

The Do Not Press, Don't Think of Tigers, 2001, ed. Peter Guttridge
Survivors'/Sixties Press, Orphans of Albion, 2006, ed. Barry Tebb
The People's Poet Anthology 2006, ed. Paula Brown
Sixties Press, Beyond Stigma, 2006, ed. Barry Tebb & Daisy Abey
Sixties Press, The Real Survivors' Anthology, 2006, ed. Barry Tebb & Daisy Abey

John Agard and Peter Guttridge and the Asham Literary Endowment Trust for a First Edition Prize in 1998; Sophie Hannah for early encouragement and guidance; Stephanie Smith-Browne, Doreen King and Munayem Mayenin of New Hope International, (the late) Martin Blyth of South, Graham High, Colin Hambrook of DADA South and Nick Wroe of the Guardian Review for their kind reviews and notices on my work; The South, West Words, Shepherd's Bush Library, The Poetry Café, Resonance fm and the George Bernard Shaw Theatre RADA for wonderful reading venues; Maureen McKarkiel and Xochitl Tuck for encouragement and commissions; Peter Holt and Robert Allwood for their commitment; Paul Murphy, David Kessel, John Horder and John O'Donoghue for their inspirational friendships; Barry Tebb for his encouragement and belief; Simon Jenner for years of guidance, friendship and metaphor-tightening; and Paula Brown for her unswerving commitment and encouragement.

Previous publications

Giving Light, Waterloo Press, 2003
Clocking-in for the Witching Hour, Sixties Press, 2004
Feed a Cold, Starve a Fever, Sixties Press, 2004
Picaresque – a play for voices, Survivors' Press, 2005

Giving Light

When women give birth, the Spanish say
They're *giving light* – and it's said
The newborn child comes into the day
Armed with a loaf of bread.